# Heinemann **Scottish** History
## for Standard Gr

John Kerr

Series editor: Jim McGonigle

# Germany
# 1918–39

**www.heinemann.co.uk**

✓ Free online support
✓ Useful weblinks
✓ 24 hour online ordering

**01865 888058**

**Heinemann**

*Inspiring generations*

Heinemann Educational Publishers
Halley Court, Jordan Hill, Oxford OX2 8EJ
Part of Harcourt Education

Heinemann is the registered trademark of
Harcourt Education Limited

© John A. Kerr, 2003

First published 2003

08 07 06 05 04 03
10 9 8 7 6 5 4 3 2 1

British Library Cataloguing in Publication Data is available
from the British Library on request.

ISBN 0 435 326937

Designed by Hicksdesign
Produced by Kamae Design, Oxford

Original illustrations © Harcourt Education Limited, 2003

Illustrated by Kamae Design, John Storey

Printed in Spain by Mateu Cromo S.A.

Cover photo: © Popperfoto

Picture research by Liz Moore

Acknowledgements
Every effort has been made to contact copyright holders of material reproduced in this book.
Any omissions will be rectified in subsequent printings if notice is given to the publishers.

l=left; r=right

page 4, Corbis/Bettmann; page 6l, Corbis; page 6r, Corbis; page 9, AKG; page 10, Source
Unknown; page 13r, AKG; page 15, Peter Newark's Pictures; page 16, AKG; page 19,
Corbis/Christel Gersrtenberg; page 24, Randall Bytwerk; page 25, Source Unknown; page 27,
AKG; page 28, Source Unknown; page 32, Hulton Getty; page 33, Corbis; page 36, AKG;
page 37, Mary Evans Picture Library; page 40, Hulton Getty; page 44, Source Unknown; page
45, Hulton Getty; page 47, AKG; page 11, Hulton; page 49, Punch Cartoon Library; page 50,
Centre for the Study of Cartoons and Caricature/Atlantis Syndication; page 51, Corbis; page
52, Getty; page 53, Atlantic Syndication; page 58l, Peter Newark's Military Picture; page 58r,
AKG; page 61, AKG; page 63, AKG; page 65l, Hulton Archive; page 65r, AKG; page 68,
Source Unknown; page 69, AKG; page 71, Popperfoto; page 74, Source Unknown; page 75,
Randall Bytwerk; page 79, AKG; page 82, Moviestore Collection; page 83, BPK; page 84,
British Library of Economics; page 85, Ullstein Bilderdienst; page 86, Mary Evans
Picture Library.

# CONTENTS

## INTRODUCTION
# The story starts here

## What's it all about?

**In this book you will learn:**

- how Germany faced many problems after its defeat in the First World War
- how these problems were often linked to the defeat in the war
- how the governments of Germany coped with these problems
- how the people of Germany were affected by these changes.

Germany was ruled by Kaiser Wilhelm II until November 1918.

The **kaiser** had led Germany into the First World War. However, by the autumn it was clear Germany was facing defeat.

On 9 November Kaiser Wilhelm II **abdicated**. The **monarchy** had ended. The government of Germany passed to politicians who had little experience of running the country.

Two days later, on 11 November 1918, an **armistice** was accepted by all sides and the fighting stopped.

### Glossary

**kaiser:** the German emperor

**abdicate:** to give up the role of ruler

**monarchy:** a country ruled by a hereditary leader, such as a king, queen or emperor

**armistice:** a temporary peace agreement between countries

**revolution:** the overthrow of a government or ruler

**republic:** a country without a monarch

Even before the end of the war, **revolution** was breaking out in Germany. Some Germans wanted fast, violent change. Others wanted slower change. Fighting broke out inside Germany between these groups. As this conflict went on, a new **republic** was born in which elected politicians governed Germany with no member of the royal family involved.

In later years, many Germans believed the new government was responsible for the country's defeat and the problems which followed – but was that fair?

### Source A

Kaiser Wilhelm II.

> 1    Use at least four of the words in the glossary box to describe what happened in Germany towards the end of 1918.

# 1   THE ROAD TO 1918

## What's it all about?

The First World War lasted from 1914 until 1918. For most of that time Germans believed they could win the war. However, by the autumn of 1918, it was obvious that Germany was about to lose the war.

### THE FIRST WORLD WAR

In 1914, Europe went to war. At its start, the First World War involved the major powers of Germany and Austria-Hungary on one side and Britain, France and Russia on the other.

If you have studied the causes of the First World War, you will have learned how growing tensions and suspicions in the years before 1914 led to the outbreak of war. You will know that each side blamed the other for starting the war.

By the end of 1914, the war had reached deadlock as neither side could achieve a quick victory. As the war spread across Europe and into Africa, Asia and the Middle East, it cost millions of lives, but even as late as the spring of 1918 each side still believed it could win.

In 1918, the German people were told that victory was just around the corner. Russia had surrendered in early 1918 and Germany felt it now had the advantage on the western front. The German army launched a massive attack in the spring of 1918 which almost won the war, but the attack failed.

The military leaders of Germany began to accept the possibility of defeat.

### WHAT PROBLEMS FACED GERMANY BY LATE 1918?

By the late summer of 1918, the German army was in serious difficulties.

The USA had recently joined the war against Germany and, in August 1918, a huge attack by **Allied forces** including British and US soldiers forced the German army to retreat.

By September, the Germans had lost one million soldiers, while the numbers of fresh, well-equipped US troops in Europe grew to over 2 million. Germany's allies – Bulgaria, Turkey and Austria-Hungary – had all surrendered and German troops were surrendering in their thousands.

## Glossary

**Allied forces:** Britain, the USA, France and Russia joined together to fight Germany – they are often called the Allies

**Source A**

A photograph of German troops in a French prison camp. German troops surrendered in their thousands.

**Source B**

The Germans are being pushed back. All along the front line, pockets of German soldiers are found hiding in shell holes and ruined buildings. They offer no resistance but surrender at once, throwing down their equipment, everything except a small sack in which are kept bread, soap and a razor. Batches of prisoners are being brought back in a steady stream. Many say they are fed up with the war.

A description of the situation in August 1918 taken from a British newspaper.

Inside Germany the people were suffering. The British navy was stopping food and other essential supplies getting to Germany. Coal was in short supply, which led to power cuts.

Food became scarce and people scavenged in fields and gutters for scraps of rotting food. Industrial production had slumped and confidence was destroyed. The health of most Germans suffered and when a flu epidemic hit Germany, thousands died.

By November 1918, Germans were exhausted. Defeat was inevitable.

**Source C**

A photograph of exhausted German troops.

1   What evidence is there that the German army faced serious problems by August 1918?

2   Describe the difficulties faced by the German people during 1918.

3   Explain why defeat was inevitable for Germany by late 1918.

## ... IN CONCLUSION

⋯⋯> Until the summer of 1918, most Germans believed they could win the war, but by the autumn, Germany faced serious problems:

■ Its army was being defeated.

■ Its allies had surrendered.

Inside Germany the civilian population was facing serious hardships. Germany was about to lose the war.

## PRACTISE YOUR ENQUIRY SKILLS

**Study the sources in this chapter carefully and answer the questions which follow. You should use your own knowledge where appropriate.**

**Source D** is taken from the autobiography of General Paul von Hindenburg, leader of the German army until October 1918.

**Source D**

> In the middle of August I did not consider that the time had come for us to give up the idea of winning the war. I fully realised what the homeland had already suffered in the way of sacrifices and difficulties and what they would possibly still have to bear. I believed that our own public would stand firm if only we at the front continued to stand firm too.

1    How fully do Sources B and C (page 6) show the problems facing Germany in the autumn of 1918?

2    Compare the evidence in this chapter about the chances of German victory in the autumn of 1918 with Hindenburg's comments about the situation in Germany (Source D).

3    Why do you think there is such a difference between the reality of the problems facing Germany in late 1918 and what Hindenburg wrote in his autobiography?

# 2 REVOLUTION AND ABDICATION

## What's it all about?

In early November 1918, revolution spread across Germany. Soldiers, sailors and civilians wanted the war to end, but the Allies would not make peace with the kaiser. Eventually, the kaiser abdicated and the German monarchy ended on 9 November 1918.

## GERMANY'S PROBLEM – HOW TO END THE WAR

Germany's military leaders knew that as long as the kaiser ruled, the victorious Allies, especially Britain and France, would want to punish Germany severely. They hoped that if they changed the government to a more **democratic system,** the Allies might not be so hard on Germany. For that reason, the German Parliament, the *Reichstag*, was given more power and a chancellor, Prince Max of Baden, was appointed.

### Glossary

**democratic system:** where the government of a country is elected by the people

Prince Max's task was to arrange a peace agreement based on a proposal made by President Wilson of the USA early in 1918. This proposal was called the Fourteen Points and aimed at a fair peace settlement. Although Germany had rejected the proposal when it thought it could still win the war, in autumn 1918 the German leadership hoped the offer was still on the table.

### Source A

*The German government accepts as a basis for the peace negotiations the programme laid down by the President of the United States of America in January 1918.*

*To avoid further bloodshed, the German government requests the president to bring about the immediate conclusion of an armistice, by land, by sea and in the air.*

**Part of a letter written by Prince Max of Baden to President Wilson on 3 October 1918.**

The USA rejected the German request. By October 1918, attitudes had hardened against Germany. The Allies wanted to punish Germany and they made it clear they would not agree to peace as long as the kaiser still ruled Germany. The kaiser would have to go.

## MUTINY!

Although the kaiser did not want to abdicate, events moved quickly and he was forced to step down.

On 28 October 1918, the German High Command decided on a final naval battle in the North Sea in order to save the honour of the German navy. They put at risk the lives of 80,000 men. This proved to be the final straw.

The sailors saw no point in fighting and probably dying when the war was all but over. They refused to take part and mutinied. The **mutiny** of sailors on two battleships based at the Kiel naval base was the spark which ignited the revolution in Germany.

The revolution spread quickly as workers' and sailors' councils took control of the naval bases at Kiel and Wilhelmshaven.

## Glossary

**mutiny:** when soldiers and sailors refuse to obey their officers

## Source B

Toward the end of October 1918, my father wrote that the High Seas Fleet was under orders to go down in battle to save the honour of High Command. Their honour is not our honour, my father wrote.

Then came stirring news. Mutiny in the Kaiser's fleet! Anxious voices cried out 'Will the fleet sail out! … No, the fleet must not sail! It's murder! Finish the war!'

**From *Out of the Night*, the autobiography of Jan Valtin, a young revolutionary published in 1941.**

## Source C

German sailors mutiny in Kiel, November 1918.

## JUST LIKE RUSSIA!

The previous year, in 1917, a revolution had overthrown the government in Russia. Ordinary working people had seized power and set up workers', soldiers' and sailors' councils, which were sometimes called by their Russian name of Soviets.

The result was that in many German towns and cities German revolutionaries set up workers' and sailors' councils to rule their areas. The authority of the kaiser and Germany's old government was collapsing. By 4 November 1918, the red flags of revolution flew over many German ships.

## THE KAISER MUST GO!

By 6 November 1918, sailors', soldiers' and workers' councils controlled the German ports of Hamburg, Bremen and Lübeck. By 8 November, many other German cities such as Dresden, Frankfurt, Cologne and Munich, were also controlled by the revolutionaries. Finally, on 9 November, workers' and soldiers' councils were set up in the capital, Berlin.

Politicians and military leaders sent urgent messages to the kaiser – 'We have done all within our power to keep the masses in check' – and urged him to abdicate.

Many Germans blamed the kaiser for the defeat in the First World War, especially when he had led them to believe that victory was just around the corner. They resented the losses and destruction caused by four years of war which had gained Germany nothing. Now they realised that as long as the kaiser was in power the Allies would continue to make Germany suffer.

1   Describe what Germany did to try to end the war by October 1918.

2   Explain why the naval mutiny was an important event.

3   Why was the kaiser so unpopular in Germany by November 1918?

## THE END OF THE MONARCHY

The commander of the German army, Groener, summed up the situation by 9 November 1918 when he said to the kaiser, 'If you won't abdicate, the best thing for you to do is shoot yourself.'

But Kaiser Wilhelm was only persuaded to abdicate when he saw law and order collapse inside Germany. He fled to Holland where he was given **political asylum**. Britain and France were angry as they felt the kaiser had escaped justice. The German monarchy had ended, but what would replace it?

### Glossary

**political asylum**: protection given by a government to foreign people who have fled their own country because of conflicts or disagreement with their government

---

### Source D

'Germany, how many will be left to enjoy the fruits of your 'victory'?' This British cartoon sums up how many Germans felt about the kaiser in 1918.

1   Describe the situation in Germany which led to the abdication of the kaiser.

2   What were the main reasons why the kaiser abdicated?

## ... IN CONCLUSION

···▷ The Allies would not make peace with Germany until the kaiser was no longer in power. When mutinies in the German navy sparked a revolution across Germany, the kaiser was forced to abdicate. The German monarchy ended on 9 November 1918.

### PRACTISE YOUR ENQUIRY SKILLS

**Study the sources in this chapter carefully and answer the questions which follow. You should use your own knowledge where appropriate.**

Source E is taken from the autobiography of Jan Valtin, a young revolutionary, who witnessed the mutiny in November 1918.

**Source E**

> That night I saw the mutinous sailors roll into Bremen in trucks – red flags ( the symbol of revolution) and machine guns mounted on them. Many of the workers were armed with guns. A frightened old woman wailed piercingly, 'What is all this? What is the world coming to?' A young worker grasped the old woman's shoulders. 'Revolution,' he laughed. 'Revolution, Madam.'

1   Why is Source E valuable evidence about Germany at the end of the war?

Source F is taken from the Abdication Proclamation of Wilhelm II on 28 November 1918.

**Source F**

> I give up for all time claims to the German Imperial throne. At the same time I release all officers and men of the navy and army from their oath of loyalty. I expect of them that until the re-establishment of order in the German Empire they shall render assistance to those in actual power in Germany, in protecting the German people from the threatening dangers of anarchy, famine and foreign rule.

2   How useful is Source F as evidence of the problems facing Germany in 1918?

3   What effect did the kaiser's abdication announcement have on the way that Germany would be governed in the future?

# 3 THE SPARTACIST RISING

## What's it all about?

When the kaiser abdicated, a new provisional government led by Friedrich Ebert, leader of the Social Democratic Party (SPD), was set up. Ebert knew there was a danger of communist revolution sweeping across Germany and, in 1919, the Spartacists, who later became known as the Communist Party or KPD, tried to start a revolution to create a communist Germany. The rising failed. Ebert had help from the army and groups of ex-soldiers, called Freikorps, who used extreme brutality to destroy the revolutionaries.

### THE PROVISIONAL GOVERNMENT

When the kaiser abdicated, there had not been time to hold elections – nor had a voting system been arranged. Ebert and the new **provisional government** had to start making these arrangements.

Germany also became a republic, but how was the new republic to be governed? How would the elected representatives be chosen?

Before Ebert could tackle these issues, he had to deal with challenges to the authority of the new government.

### Glossary

provisional government: a temporary government which governs until a permanent government can be set up

### WHAT DID EBERT AND THE SPD WANT FOR GERMANY?

Ebert was against violent revolution. When asked his opinion about the changes in Germany at the end of the war, he said, 'I do not want revolution – in fact I hate it like sin.'

Ebert wanted to create a democratic Germany where people would elect representatives who would work in the *Reichstag* to pass laws to help the German people. He wanted open discussion in the *Reichstag* between groups who had different aims, but at least the people's voice would be heard through their representatives.

However, there were groups in Germany who wanted faster change, using violence if necessary. One newspaper reported in early November, 'The revolution is on the march: What happened in Kiel will spread throughout Germany.' Ebert feared that might be true.

### WHO WERE THE SPARTACISTS?

Spartacists were communists who wanted to overthrow the provisional government. They named themselves after a Roman slave and gladiator called Spartacus who had led a revolt against the Roman Empire. The slaves wanted a revolution to make their lives better – so Spartacus was a hero who inspired many German revolutionaries.

During the First World War, the Spartacists had protested against the war and many of their leaders were put in prison, but in October 1918, **Chancellor** Max of Baden released the Spartacists. They immediately began to plan for a revolution. The scene was set for conflict between the moderate, slower, gradual ideas of Ebert and the revolutionary Spartacists.

## WHAT DID THEY WANT?

Spartacists wanted to destroy 'old' Germany and transfer power to the working classes. This cartoon shows that the Kaiser had gone but other targets remained.

### Glossary

**chancellor:** senior minister, similar to the British prime minister

**National Assembly:** parliament

The Spartacists wanted the working classes to control society. They did not want to work through parliamentary discussion because they believed the upper classes would use their power in the *Reichstag* to block reforms of benefit to the working classes.

One of the Spartacist demands was 'Abolish all parliaments and transfer all power to the workers' and soldiers' councils!' The Spartacists were prepared to use violence to achieve their aims.

The government's reaction was to issue posters which showed Spartacists as violent, anti-democratic terrorists while the **National Assembly** – or parliament – was shown as protecting the people of Germany.

### Source A

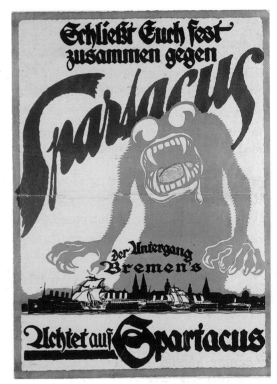

A German government poster showing the Spartacists as monsters. The poster says 'Beware of Spartacus'.

1   Describe the main differences between the Spartacists and the Social Democrats led by Ebert.

2   Describe the content of Source A in detail.

3   Explain how you think the artist who drew Source A felt about the Social Democratic Party and the Spartacists.

## PREPARATION FOR CONFLICT

Ebert knew he needed a powerful force to help him defeat the challenge of the revolutionaries in Germany. At first, he turned to the German army. On the evening of 10 November 1918, Ebert struck a deal with General Groener, chief of the army. Ebert promised to do nothing to harm the interests of the army if Groener and his troops would crush the revolution and defend Ebert's government.

### Source B

Ten divisions were to march into Berlin to take power from the workers' and soldiers' councils. Ebert was in agreement with this … we worked out a programme for cleaning up Berlin and the disarming of the Spartacists.

**General Groener described the plan agreed with Ebert in his diary on November 10 1918.**

Ebert had also appointed a politician called Gustav Noske as minister for defence. Noske immediately began forming volunteer units of loyal anti-revolutionary ex-soldiers called the *Freikorps*.

## WHO WERE THE *FREIKORPS*?

The *Freikorps* were groups of experienced, battle-hardened and heavily armed volunteer ex-soldiers. They believed that Germany had lost the war because it had been betrayed – or 'stabbed in the back' – by communists and revolutionaries. The *Freikorps* wanted revenge!

At first, the *Freikorps* were recruited to protect Germany in case communists from Russia invaded, but soon they were used in the streets of Berlin against the Spartacists.

### ⋯⋮ Activity

Look at the grid below. Ebert, the *Freikorps* and the Spartacists are at the top. Now look at the six statements below the grid. Your task is to copy the grid and then sort out the statements provided so that they show clearly what each person or group did and did not want. Watch out – one statement is repeated. It is not a mistake!

|  | Ebert | *Freikorps* | Spartacists |
|---|---|---|---|
| What this person/ group wanted |  |  |  |
| What this person/ group did not want |  |  |  |

A communist revolution
The power of the upper classes and army officers to stay the same
The needs of workers and soldiers to be ignored
Laws to be made by the *Reichstag*
To use violence to overthrow the *Reichstag* and start a communist revolution
A communist revolution

## Source C

This picture shows members of the *Freikorps* armed with flame-throwers in January 1919. The *Freikorps* were used to attack the Spartacists.

## THE SPARTACIST REVOLT

The government had been expecting an attempted revolution led by the Spartacists and had made plans to cope with it.

In early January 1919, a 'peaceful demonstration' attended by 100,000 people in Berlin turned violent. Spartacist supporters took over the centre of Berlin, but they had made no organised plans for armed revolution. Their leaders spent hours discussing what to do next while 200,000 armed workers waited for orders outside in the freezing streets. Revolutionary workers became tired and started to return home. Even before the *Freikorps* soldiers entered the city, the Spartacists had lost most of their strength. Then the killing began.

Within a week – known as 'Bloody Week' – the revolution was over. The *Freikorps* crushed the Spartacists. On 15 January, Spartacist leaders Karl Liebknecht and Rosa Luxemburg were arrested. Both were taken to *Freikorps* headquarters for 'investigation'. Liebknecht was the first to be taken out and shot, 'while trying to escape'. Rosa Luxemburg's body was dumped in an icy canal. It was not discovered until the end of May. Almost 700 men and women were captured and executed by the *Freikorps*.

The new German republic had got off to a bloody start and this had important consequences for democracy in Germany. The communists never trusted the socialists again. Ten years later, when Hitler was rising to power, the hatred felt by the communists towards the SPD for destroying the Spartacist rising prevented them uniting against Hitler in elections.

1   Explain why Ebert made a secret deal with the German army.

2   Describe the main events of the Spartacist rising.

3   Why did the Spartacist rising fail?

4   Explain the importance of the Spartacist rising to the new German republic.

## ... IN CONCLUSION

The provisional government did not want a revolution. However, the Spartacists wanted to bring about change more quickly and planned to overthrow the government. Ebert used ex-soldiers called *Freikorps* to crush the Spartacist rising. Socialists and communists never again cooperated in Germany.

*PRACTISE YOUR ENQUIRY SKILLS*

**Study the sources in this chapter carefully and answer the questions which follow. You should use your own knowledge where appropriate.**

**Source D** describes the events of 12 January 1919.

**Source D**

> The Spartacists have been defeated in their attempt to take over Berlin. Troops loyal to the government along with *Freikorps* soldiers combined to defeat the revolt. There was much confused fighting in the streets. The revolt collapsed when 3000 *Freikorps* men marched into the city yesterday and the Spartacists, whose call for support from German workers had been mostly ignored, faded away. (Adapted from the *Chronicle of the 20th Century*)

1    How fully does Source D describe the main events of the Spartacist rising in 1919?

**Source E** is taken from a German newspaper of 1919.

**Source E**

> The deaths of Rosa Luxemburg and Liebknecht were the proper reward for the blood bath they unleashed. The result of her own actions killed the woman. The day of judgement of Luxemburg and Liebknecht is over. Germany can breathe again. The Spartacists were criminals pure and simple.

2    Identify and explain the attitude of the writer of Source E to the Spartacists.

**Source F**

**Source F** was drawn by a communist artist. A *Freikorps* officer is celebrating his victory and saying 'Cheers, Noske, the young revolution is dead.'

3    Why was Source F drawn? You should use your own knowledge and give reasons for your answer.

4    How can you tell from the cartoon that the artist was an opponent of the *Freikorps*?

# 4 THE WEIMAR CONSTITUTION

## What's it all about?

Weimar Germany or the Weimar Republic refers to a time between 1919 and 1933 when Germany was a republic ruled by elected representatives. There was also a set of rules called a constitution which laid down the rights and duties that citizens of the new Germany had.

## WHY WAS IT CALLED 'WEIMAR' GERMANY?

In early 1919, a National Assembly was elected by the German people. Its job was to write a **constitution**.

The National Assembly moved away from the violent atmosphere of Berlin to the town of Weimar. During the late eighteenth and early nineteenth centuries, Weimar was the heart of German culture. But in 1919, Weimar was, most importantly, safe and peaceful.

The politicians who met at Weimar wanted to create a new democratic form of government for Germany which would be fair to all people. They also wanted to make sure that decisions could be taken quickly if Germany ever again faced revolution.

### Glossary

**constitution**: set of basic rules about how a country should be governed and the rights people should have

**German federation**: Germany was made up of different states, each with its own local government

**cabinet minister**: politician in charge of a government department

## POWER TO THE PEOPLE!

The first part (or article) in the constitution stated, 'The **German Federation** is a republic. Supreme power comes from the people.'

Article 125 gave more details about what power the people had: 'The representatives are elected by all men and women over 20 years of age', but you had to be 35 or over to vote in presidential elections.

Although the president had the power to hand out important jobs such as chancellor and **cabinet ministers**, these people could be removed by the *Reichstag*, which was elected by the people. So it looked like ordinary voters would have power in the new Germany.

To make the political system even fairer, a voting system of proportional representation was used. Political parties gained a number of representatives in the *Reichstag* based on their share of votes at the election. Even small parties which gained relatively few votes gained some seats in the *Reichstag*.

## BASIC CIVIL RIGHTS

The German people now not only had the right to choose the politicians who represented them. The new constitution also guaranteed their basic rights, called Fundamental Laws. Here are some of them:

---

**Fundamental Laws**

Article 109. All Germans are equal before the law.

Article 114. Personal freedom is inviolable. No restraint or deprivation of personal liberty by the public power is admissible, unless authorised by law.

Article 115. The residence of every German is a sanctuary for him and inviolable.

Article 116. No one may be punished for an act unless such act was legally punishable at the time when it was committed.

Article 117. The secrecy of correspondence, as well as the secrecy of postal and telephonic communications, is inviolable.

Article 118. Every German is entitled within the limits of the general law freely to express his opinions by word of mouth, writing, printing, pictorial representation, or otherwise. Laws are also permitted for the purpose of combating pornographic publications.

Article 124. All Germans have the right to form societies or associations for any object that does not run counter to the criminal law ... The same provisions apply to religious societies and bodies.

---

## NATIONAL AND LOCAL GOVERNMENT

Germany was made up of different states and each state looked after its own local government. In the new political set-up, while the *Reichstag* represented the people of Germany, the Reichsrat represented the interests of the different states in Germany.

---

### ⋯⋰ *Activity*

Read all the information in this box and working with a partner:

Design a graphic which shows clearly why the Weimar constitution is still thought to be a real attempt at creating a fair society.

What's the reason for doing this?
Later in this book, you will look at the laws introduced by the Nazis.
They deliberately destroyed the basic rights given to people in the Weimar constitution. You will be able to see clearly the contrast between Weimar democracy and Nazi dictatorship.

- How do we do this? Read the relevant articles from the constitution.

- Decide, using a dictionary and asking advice if necessary, what the articles really mean and how they help in creating a fair society.

- Agree with your partner on a sentence which rewrites the meaning of each article in a form of words you understand.

- Plan an image or cartoon which illustrates the point made by each article.

- Use your images and sentences in a larger diagram under the title 'The Weimar constitution – a fair democracy'.

## WAS THE NEW DEMOCRATIC CONSTITUTION PERFECT?

The Weimar Republic has been called 'the most perfect democracy ... on paper'. What does that mean? Quite simply, the constitution had flaws in it which could be exploited by groups that wanted to destroy the republic.

### The voting system created difficulties

The voting system was based on proportional representation and, although fair, could be confusing and lead to political instability.

There was never a clear winner at elections. Even the party that won most seats in the *Reichstag* and therefore had most deputies (like our MPs) could be outvoted by smaller parties uniting against it. Deals had to be done between parties and **coalition governments** set up. These coalition governments were unlikely to put into action strong, decisive policies.

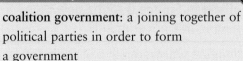

### Glossary

**coalition government:** a joining together of political parties in order to form a government

### The fair system gave its enemies respectability

The system of proportional voting also allowed small, extremist parties to gain some representation in the *Reichstag* – even if these parties intended to destroy the new republic.

### Source A

A German Communist party poster. The red working-class figure is saying 'Enough of this system' – the same system the party was asking people to vote in!

This led to a lot of confusion for the German people in the 1920s. They were unclear about who made up their government or how long it would last. Weimar politics were unstable and led to discontent among the people, who seldom got what they voted for. For many 'middle of the road' democratic parties, it was often a balancing act trying to prevent one side or the other having too much power.

### Was too much power in the hands of the president?

The writers of the constitution realised that future crises might occur and so Article 48 gave the president, who was elected every seven years, the power to rule in an emergency without needing approval from the *Reichstag*.

## THE HUMILIATION OF VERSAILLES

In June 1919, Germany signed the **Treaty of Versailles** (see Chapter 5). German representatives had no choice but to sign, but many Germans blamed the new Weimar government for this humiliation. There was already a loss of confidence in the republic.

From the outset, the Weimar Republic also suffered from a lack of support within Germany. Many important Germans remained loyal to the empire. German army officers claimed that Germany had been defeated by the revolution, not by the Allied armies. Other Germans who had enjoyed a comfortable life and the respect of others before the war resented power being handed over to people they saw as less important (see Source B).

Many influential people were suspicious and resentful of the new government.

### Source B

Democracy! There was no democracy when Germany was great under the kaiser. Now Germany's leaders must listen to the voice of

### Glossary

**Treaty of Versailles:** the peace treaty, signed in June 1919, which officially ended the First World War. The treaty punished Germany for the deaths and destruction of the war.

every shopkeeper and farm labourer, along with their women. The backbone of Germany is its landowners and its army officers. They alone should have power!

An ex-army officer writing in a letter to his brother in 1919.

Would these previously influential people try to help make the new Germany work? Or would they undermine confidence in the new democracy? Would the extremist parties in Germany try to destabilise the new government?

The horse in this cartoon represents the Weimar Republic. 'Who are these fellows they've put on my back?' he asks. The fellows are the extremist parties struggling to take control.

1  What is the attitude of the ex-army officer in Source B to the new democratic government?

2  Imagine you were alive in 1920 and you were against the new system of government. Write a short statement about the same length as Source B. In your statement try to include two more complaints about the new political system and why you think the new ideas will not work.

3  Explain the difficulties facing the new Weimar Republic which are suggested in the cartoon above.

## ... IN CONCLUSION

···> The German republic was called Weimar Germany after the town where the new constitution was written. The Weimar constitution tried to be fair to everyone, but it had serious weaknesses:

■ The *Reichstag* contained political parties which wanted to destroy it.

■ Proportional representation meant there was never a clear winner at elections.

Many Germans were unsure and suspicious of the new democratic government.

*PRACTISE YOUR ENQUIRY SKILLS*

**Study the sources in this chapter carefully and answer the questions which follow. You should use your own knowledge where appropriate.**

**Source D** is taken from a German newspaper in 1920.

**Source D**

The new constitution is to be welcomed. For the first time the ordinary people have a political voice that really counts. They also have guarantees of their freedom, freedom to vote, freedom to have opinions, the right to be free from political interference in their lives. The Reichstag is an expression of what the people want. Laws will be fair to everyone and all opinions will be represented in the *Reichstag*.

**Source E** is taken from a statement made by an opponent of the new democracy.

**Source E**

The new constitution has serious weaknesses. The new *Reichstag* will achieve little if anything. Extreme groups enter it intending to destroy it. The people have but a small voice with each opinion being cancelled by an opposing one. No clear decisions are made since no single party has the power to put its policies into action.

1    Compare the views about the Weimar constitution contained in Sources D and E.

**Source F** comes from the diary of Princess Blücher, a British woman married to a German nobleman, written in December 1918.

**Source F**

The socialists have not had time to develop a really strong government, or to test the practical working of their theories about government. I believe the German people need something for their imagination – a leader who represents the ideal. There is no attraction in a short, stout president with a bald head, top hat and a black coat.

2    What is the attitude of Princess Blücher towards the new German government?

3    How reliable as historical evidence do you think her opinions are?

# 5 GERMANY AND THE TREATY OF VERSAILLES

## What's it all about?

On 28 June 1919, the Treaty of Versailles officially ended the First World War and it punished Germany severely. Once the terms of the peace treaty were given to the German representatives, they had a simple choice – either accept the treaty or Germany would be invaded. Most Germans were angry about this and were anxious for revenge, an important factor used by Hitler in his rise to power many years later.

## THE MAIN TERMS OF THE TREATY

Germany's military power was reduced. It had to:

- cut its army to 100,000 men
- reduce its navy to six warships
- melt down all wartime guns and weapons into scrap metal.

Germany was not allowed:

- to have **conscription**
- to have submarines
- to have an air force
- to have tanks
- to make an alliance with Austria
- to have soldiers or military equipment in the Rhineland, a large part of western Germany that borders Holland, Belgium and France.

Germany's economic and industrial power was reduced. It had to:

- give some of its land to Belgium, France, Denmark and Poland
- hand over all of its colonies (territory belonging to Germany in other parts of the world)
- agree to pay **reparations** to the Allies for the damage caused by the war

- be split into two parts. East Prussia was separated from the rest of Germany by the 'Polish Corridor', a big strip of land given to the new country of Poland.

Finally, Germany had to sign the 'war guilt' clause, which meant it had to accept that it had caused not only the war but also the deaths and destruction resulting from the war. Most Germans felt humiliated.

### Glossary

**conscription:** calling up recruits to the armed forces

**reparations:** compensation or financial payments

## HOW DID GERMANS REACT TO THE TREATY?

The German people believed that since the kaiser and his government had gone, there was no reason why they should not be treated fairly and offered a fresh start.

They hoped that a negotiated peace would be agreed on. However, when they heard about the treaty, most Germans were shocked and angry. They called the treaty a *Diktat* – a dictated treaty that was forced on them.

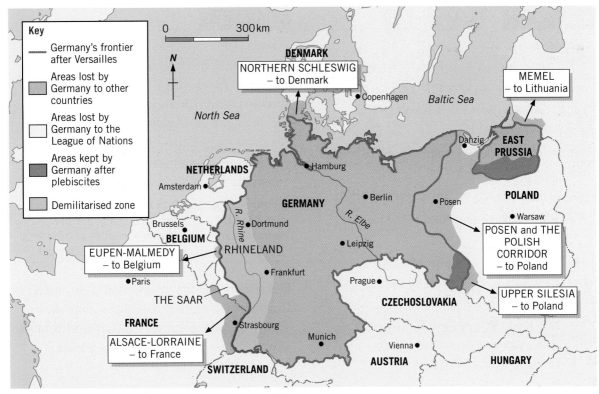

A map showing how the Treaty of Versailles redrew the map of Germany.

## Source A

*We had come to Versailles in the expectation of receiving the peace which has been promised us ... Instead a whole nation is called upon to sign its own death warrant.*

**A member of the German delegation sent to Versailles described his reaction when he saw the terms of the treaty.**

Many Germans blamed the new government. They did not believe that the German army had been defeated in 1918. After all, Germany had not been invaded. Some Germans called members of the new German government 'November criminals' who had betrayed Germany and 'stabbed Germany in the back', once by accepting the armistice in November 1918 and again by signing the Treaty of Versailles. In fact, one of the politicians who signed the armistice, Matthias Erzberger, was later murdered by a gang who blamed the new government for all of Germany's problems.

## WAS GERMANY STABBED IN THE BACK?

Germany's army was defeated by the Allies. If Germany had not accepted the armistice, the Allies would have invaded Germany.

Regardless of the truth about Germany's defeat and exhaustion in 1918, many Germans continued to link the republic with defeat and humiliation. The Treaty of Versailles is an important part of why many people distrusted the new democratic government.

## MOST GERMANS WANTED REVENGE

Germany's reaction was clear, even on the day the treaty was signed (see Source B). Only a few people realised that Germany had no choice but to sign the treaty and accept its demands.

## Source B

Vengeance!

Today at Versailles a disgraceful treaty is being signed. Never forget it!

Today German honour is dragged to the grave. Never forget it !

The German people will push forward to regain their pride.

We will have revenge for the shame of 1919!

From a German newspaper, 28 June 1919.

1    Describe the reaction of most Germans to the Treaty of Versailles.

2    What was the German newspaper's reaction to the treaty (Source B)? Use evidence from the source to support your answer.

## Source C

People were ready here to make reparation for the wrong done by their leaders, but now they say that Wilson (the American president) has broken his word and an undying hate is in the heart of every German. Over and over again I hear the same words, 'We shall hate our conquerors with a hatred that will only cease when the day of our revenge comes again.'

From *An English Wife in Berlin* (1920), the autobiography of Princess Blücher, a British woman married to a German nobleman. She was living in Germany when the treaty was signed.

Despite the reality of the situation, many Germans continued to believe that the Treaty of Versailles was unfair and that the new German government was partly responsible for the disaster.

The myth of the 'November criminals' who 'stabbed Germany in the back' was exploited by the Nazis in their rise to power. In 1933, Adolf Hitler said, 'I will make Germany great again but before that happens the Treaty of Versailles must be destroyed.'

## Source D

Germany saw itself with its limited army of 100,000 men surrounded by threatening neighbours.

## Source E

What could we do? What was the alternative to not signing? The German people wanted peace, they were exhausted. Not to sign would mean occupation of the most important territories, the blockade continued, unemployment, hunger, the death of thousands, the holding back of our war prisoners – a catastrophe which would force us to sign more humiliating conditions.

From Toni Sender's, *The Autobiography of a German Rebel*, published in 1940.

1  According to Source E on page 24, what would have happened to Germany if it had refused to accept the treaty?

2  For what reasons did Germans dislike the Treaty of Versailles?

3  What were the short- and long-term effects of the Treaty of Versailles on Germany?

## ... IN CONCLUSION

⟶ The Treaty of Versailles reduced Germany's military, economic and industrial power. Germany also had to accept guilt for the deaths and destruction caused by the war and to agree to pay reparations. Many Germans were angry that Germany had signed such a humiliating treaty and vowed revenge. They blamed the politicians of the Weimar Republic for agreeing to the treaty and this led to discontent with the new republic.

### PRACTISE YOUR ENQUIRY SKILLS

**Study the sources in this chapter carefully and answer the questions which follow. You should use your own knowledge where appropriate.**

1  How fully does the evidence in Source B (page 24) explain reasons for the German resentment of the Treaty of Versailles?

2  Compare the attitudes towards the treaty in Sources C and E (page 24).

Horror stories and silent movies about vampires were very popular around 1919. **Source F** shows the French prime minister, Clemenceau, in the role of vampire sucking the blood of Germany. On the bedside table is a German military helmet and a shield with a German emblem.

**Source F**

3  From the evidence in Source F, how can you tell this cartoon is about the Treaty of Versailles?

4  How useful is this source as evidence of German reaction to the Treaty of Versailles?

# 6 REPARATIONS AND INFLATION, 1923

## What's it all about?

By 1923, France believed Germany was trying to avoid paying reparations and so French and Belgian troops invaded the Ruhr area of Germany to force Germany to pay up. As a result of the invasion, Germany's economy collapsed. German money lost its value and once again Germans blamed their own government for being weak and powerless.

## REPARATIONS

There were two main reasons why Germany had to pay reparations.

- The victorious Allies, especially France and Belgium, wanted compensation to rebuild their damaged countries.

- The French believed that their own safety depended on keeping Germany weak, as a weakened Germany would not be able to attack France.

By 1921, Germany was faced with the final bill for reparations. It totalled £6,600,000 to be paid in regular instalments. Reparations were also to be paid in goods as well as money so that France received 5000 trains, 150,000 railway wagons, 10,000 lorries and 140,000 cows.

## WHY DID FRENCH AND BELGIAN TROOPS INVADE THE RUHR?

A map showing the Rhineland and the Ruhr.

By the end of 1922, Germany had failed to pay several instalments of reparations on time. In January 1923, France and Belgium reacted by occupying the Ruhr region in western Germany. The Ruhr was Germany's industrial heart, producing 80 per cent of its steel and 71 per cent of its coal.

## WHAT HAPPENED WHEN THE FRENCH AND BELGIANS INVADED?

The invaders took over coal mines, steel works and factories. France intended to force Germany to pay up or work under French control. The Germans were in no position to fight back. They did not have the military strength and the Ruhr was in the Rhineland, the **demilitarised** area of Germany. Instead, German workers in the Ruhr put up passive resistance and refused to cooperate with the French and Belgian invaders. They went on strike.

### Source A

The action of the French government in the Ruhr area is a gross violation of international law and of the Treaty of Versailles.
The German government therefore orders all its officials not to obey the instructions of the occupying forces.

Statement issued by the German government in February 1923.

1   Explain fully why France and Belgium invaded the Ruhr.

2   According to Source A, how did the German government react to the Ruhr invasion?

### Glossary

**demilitarise:** to remove military forces from an area

### Source B

This German poster shows French soldiers trying to force a German worker who is on strike. He is saying, 'No, you can't force me.'

### ⋯ Activity

In Source B, the cartoonist has drawn several things relevant to the Ruhr invasion, including:

- a German worker with hands in his pockets

- French army helmets and French rifles and bayonets pointing at the worker

- working tools lying on the ground

- the word 'Nein' (German for 'No').

For each of the listed items in the cartoon, explain what point the cartoonist is trying to make about the invasion of the Ruhr.

With industrial production in the Ruhr at a standstill, Germany was producing almost nothing. Yet the German government printed more and more money to pay the strikers. The economy collapsed and **hyperinflation** hit Germany.

### Glossary

hyperinflation: a rapid rise in the level of prices of goods and services (usually daily and sometimes even hourly)

## WHAT IS HYPERINFLATION?

Since the First World War, the value of German money had been falling, meaning that prices rose as money lost its value. The French invasion of the Ruhr made the situation worse.

During 1923, with almost no wealth being created in Germany, the currency became worthless. As demand for things went up and supply of those things dried up, prices rocketed upwards.

A story in the British newspaper, the *Daily Express*, in February 1923, illustrated the uselessness of German money. A Berlin couple who were about to celebrate their golden wedding received an official letter advising them that the mayor would call and present them with a donation of money. The next morning the mayor arrived at the couple's house, and solemnly handed over a total of 1 billion marks – equal to one half penny of UK money at the time.

Worthless paper money was used for more practical purposes. A university student remembered, 'Many inflation banknotes which a few weeks before represented a huge fortune were used after October 1923 by hard-up students as toilet paper.'

1 Explain in your own words what hyperinflation means.

2 Identify the important features in source C. Explain why they are included and what point is being made about hyperinflation.

## HOW WERE THE GERMAN PEOPLE AFFECTED BY HYPERINFLATION?

Almost overnight the life savings of many Germans became worthless and they were forced to sell their valuables to buy food. Some workers were paid twice a day and could spend their wages instantly, but people who were paid monthly or depended on savings suffered because these could not keep up with price rises.

Pensioners, disabled people, the unemployed and war widows lived on fixed incomes. They always received the same amount of money each week. These incomes might have been fixed a few years before and were now worth nothing. They faced homelessness and starvation.

### Source C

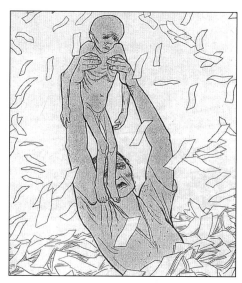

This cartoon, drawn in 1923 in *Simplicimuss* magazine, shows a German woman drowning in a sea of paper money, crying 'Bread, bread'.

However, not everyone lost out. People who owned large businesses or property profited from hyperinflation. They took out huge loans to buy property or invest in their businesses, knowing that in a few months their repayments would be worth almost nothing.

## WHAT EFFECT DID THE ECONOMIC CRISIS HAVE ON THE GERMAN GOVERNMENT?

Hyperinflation undermined confidence in the democratic government and increased discontent.

Many of the working classes supported communism, while many of the wealthy wished for the return of the 'good old days' of the kaiser. Neither side liked the new democracy.

Middle-class people and workers lost faith in the Weimar Republic and the democratic system. As far as they were concerned, if the republic could not maintain public order and economic stability, then they would take their votes elsewhere. In years to come, when the economic crisis was over, Germans were terrified that hyperinflation would return. The economic problems of 1923 have been described as being like a scar that never healed.

When the next financial disaster struck six years later in 1929, the middle classes feared a return to the disasters of 1923. They listened to the one man who promised them safety and security – Adolf Hitler.

## WAS IT FAIR TO BLAME THE GOVERNMENT?

The roots of the economic collapse go back to the First World War. Germany had hoped that when it won the war, it would force Britain and France to pay compensation which would then be used by Germany to pay for its war costs. But when Germany lost the war, the economy was in a mess and inflation was already a problem long before 1923.

As far as most Germans were concerned, the cause of their problems was the Weimar Republic. After all, they had accepted the Treaty of Versailles, which seemed to make Germany poor and almost defenceless. Germany had been invaded and the economy was in chaos.

> 1  How did the Ruhr invasion and hyperinflation affect the way German people felt about their government?

## HOW DID HYPERINFLATION END?

The German economic collapse ended when the USA helped Germany by giving it huge loans through the Dawes Plan (see Chapter 9) to help build up the economy.

In 1924, the French left the Ruhr and a new German currency, the Rentenmark, was issued.

With the loans of money from the USA, Germany recovered and a time of political and economic stability followed. But what would happen if US money was suddenly withdrawn from Germany?

## ... IN CONCLUSION

⋯⋯> French and Belgian troops invaded the Ruhr in 1923 and, as a result, the German economy collapsed. In the crisis that followed, Germany suffered from hyperinflation when money became worthless. The hyperinflation crisis caused many Germans to blame their own government. The economy recovered thanks to loans from the USA.

*PRACTISE YOUR ENQUIRY SKILLS*

**Study the sources in this chapter carefully and answer the questions which follow. You should use your own knowledge where appropriate.**

**Source D** is taken from the personal memoirs of Frieda Wunderlich, who lived through the hyperflation crisis.

**Source D**

> As soon as I received my salary I rushed out to buy the daily necessities. My daily salary, as editor of the magazine *Soziale Praxis*, was just enough to buy one loaf of bread and a small piece of cheese or some oatmeal. On one occasion I had to refuse to give a lecture at a Berlin city college because I could not be sure my fee would cover the subway fare to the classroom and it was too far to walk. On another occasion a private lesson I gave was paid somewhat better – by one loaf of bread for the hour.

1    How useful is Source D for finding out about the effects of hyperinflation on the German people?

2    Look again at Sources B and C (pages 27–28). How useful are the cartoons for finding out about the invasion of the Ruhr and its consequences?

3    How useful are cartoons generally as historical evidence?

# 7    THE MUNICH PUTSCH

## What's it all about?

In November 1923, a nationalist group called the National Socialist German Workers' Party tried to seize power in Munich, a town in the southern German state of Bavaria. The initial letters of the party were NSDAP – these were shortened to the nickname 'Nazi'.

The Nazi leader, Adolf Hitler, intended to overthrow the Weimar Republic. The Nazis' attempt to seize power was called the Munich Putsch. It is sometimes known as the Beer Hall Putsch because the attempt to seize power started in a Munich beer hall. The putsch failed and Hitler spent a short time in prison.

### Glossary

**putsch:** a German word meaning an armed take-over of power

As you have read, in the autumn of 1923, hyperinflation was destroying the lives of thousands of Germans. In an attempt to solve the problem, the German government agreed to negotiate with the French and start paying reparations again. It seemed to be the only way to get the French out of the Ruhr and bring hyperinflation under control. However, to many Germans this looked like surrender once again.

### PLANNING THE PUTSCH

Adolf Hitler, leader of the Nazi Party, believed the time was right to start a revolution to overthrow the government.

By November 1923, the Nazis had thousands of members – some reports say as many as 50,000. These people had joined the Nazis hoping for action against the 'November criminals' who had 'stabbed Germany in the back' (see Chapter 5). Hitler knew his supporters were demanding action. He had been told by a Nazi organiser in Munich, 'Our members in Munich are becoming very restless. If nothing happens now, the men will melt away.'

Hitler wanted to overthrow the national government, but first he needed to establish his power in Bavaria, a state in southern Germany. His chance came on the night of 8 November 1923. Hitler heard that an important Bavarian politician, Gustav von Kahr, had arranged a big meeting in the Buergerbräukeller, a huge beer hall in Munich. Along with von Kahr would be General Otto von Lossow, the head of the army in Bavaria, and Colonel Hans von Seisser, commander of the state police. These three men were the most powerful people in Bavaria at that time and their support was vital if Hitler was to be successful. It was too good an opportunity to miss.

## Source A

Hitler's men gathering for the march through Munich on 8 November 1923.

> 1    Explain why Hitler chose to start a revolution in late 1923.

## THE PUTSCH

Soon after the meeting started, Hitler and 600 of his supporters went into the beer hall and lined the sides of the large room. Some witnesses say that Hitler climbed on to a platform and fired shots in the air. He claimed, 'The National Revolution has begun!' and that Nazis had already taken over important buildings in Munich. However, Hitler knew that the success of his actions depended on what von Kahr, von Seisser and von Lossow did next.

First, Hitler ordered the three men to go into a private room away from the crowd. Nobody really knows what happened in the room, but it seems likely that the three men refused to support Hitler. They only changed their minds when General

Ludendorff, a respected war hero, was brought to the beer hall, apparently to show his support for the Nazis.

Hitler made another speech to the crowd. He promised 'to know neither rest nor peace until the November criminals had been overthrown, until on the ruins of the Germany of today there should have arisen once more a Germany of power and greatness, of freedom and splendour'.

Hitler also gave the impression that von Kahr, von Seisser and von Lossow now supported the Nazis. With Ludendorff also supporting the Nazis, it looked like success was guaranteed.

## SO HOW DID IT ALL GO WRONG?

Hitler was called away from the beer hall to sort out problems in another part of Munich where German soldiers were fighting Nazis. While Hitler was away, von Kahr, von Lossow and von Seisser promised Ludendorff they would support Hitler and left the building. Once they were free, they immediately began to plan a fight back against the Nazis. Von Kahr issued a statement against Hitler saying, 'Statements forced from me, General von Lassow and Colonel von Seisser by pistol point are null and void. If the senseless and purposeless attempt at revolt had succeeded, Germany would have been plunged into chaos and Bavaria with it.'

Hitler feared the Nazi revolution was falling apart, but Ludendorff argued that if the Nazis marched into the centre of Munich, they could attract public support and, with Ludendorff at the head of the march, the army would never dare fire on them. Hitler had little choice. If he did nothing, the Nazis would lose all credibility.

On the morning of 9 November 1923 about 3000 Nazis marched behind Hitler and Ludendorff. When they entered a narrow street, armed police were at the other end, blocking their path. Nobody knows who fired the first shot, but soon shots rang out from both sides. According to different reports, between fourteen and sixteen Nazis and three policemen died during the Putsch.

Although the shooting lasted less than a minute, the Putsch was over. Hitler escaped from the scene but was soon captured along with Ludendorff and others. They were to stand trial for attempting to overthrow the government.

> ...∵ **Activity**
>
> Work with a partner.
>
> ■ Read carefully the story of the Munich Putsch. Discuss and agree what were the main events of the day in chronological order. Now write as a bullet point list the events you have agreed on.
>
> ■ Colour your list with one colour indicating when things were going well for the Nazis and another colour when things went badly.

## THE END OF THE NAZIS?

With the collapse of the Beer Hall Putsch, most people believed that Hitler and the Nazis were finished. But the trial gave Hitler and the Nazis much needed national publicity. During the trial Hitler explained how he had acted to save Germany from a weak government. He was also photographed standing beside Ludendorff, which made people think that Hitler was an important person. People began to ask who the Nazis were and what they stood for.

## HITLER'S PUNISHMENT

Just a few years before the Munich Putsch, Spartacists who had tried to overthrow the government had been murdered for the same crime Hitler was now accused of. However, when Hitler was found guilty, he was given a short prison sentence of five years in Lansberg prison.

**Source B**

Hitler in Lansberg prison. Hitler is on the far left of the photograph.

During his time in prison Hitler was free to think and plan. He also wrote a book, *Mein Kampf* (My Struggle), which was a combination of autobiography, his political ideas and his plans for the future. As it turned out, he was released in less than a year. Why was Hitler treated so leniently? It looked as if Hitler had friends in important positions.

> 1  Describe the aims of the Nazis and their methods during the Munich Putsch.
>
> 2  Describe the immediate and longer-term effects of the failure of the Munich Putsch for Hitler and the Nazis.
>
> 3  Explain the importance of the Munich Putsch to the Nazi Party.

## ... IN CONCLUSION

⇢ The Nazis tried to take power in November 1923. The Putsch started in a beer hall in Munich. It failed, but the trial got big publicity and Hitler became a nationally known political leader. Although Hitler was sent to prison, he was not seriously punished, which suggested that powerful people in Germany sympathised with Nazi ideas.

### PRACTISE YOUR ENQUIRY SKILLS

**Study the sources in this chapter carefully and answer the questions which follow. You should use your own knowledge where appropriate.**

**Source C** is part of the speech Hitler made at the Munich beer hall, on 8 November 1923.

**Source C**

> The government of the November Criminals and the Reich President are declared to be removed. I propose that, until accounts have been finally settled with the November Criminals, the direction of policy in the national government be taken over by me.

1     How valuable is Source C as evidence of Hitler's reasons for starting the Munich Putsch?

**Sources D** and **E** both describe Hitler's actions on 9 November 1923 when the Putsch failed.

**Source D** is taken from a book written by Rudolf Olden called *Hitler the Pawn* (1936).

**Source D**

> Hitler wanted 'to make himself scarce'. General Ludendorff had another plan. No German, at any rate no German in uniform, would shoot at the 'General of the World War', at the national hero. At about noon a procession of 2000 National Socialists marched, twelve abreast, through the town. At the first shot Hitler had flung himself to the ground. He sprained his arm, but this did not prevent him from running. He found his car and drove into the mountains.

**Source E** is taken from the official biography of Adolf Hitler published by the Nazi Party in 1934.

**Source E**

> Hitler shouted, 'Close the ranks,' and linked arms with his neighbours. The body of the man with whom Hitler was linked shot up into the air like a ball, tearing Hitler's arm with him, so that it sprang from the joint and fell back limp and dead. Hitler approached the man and stooped over him. Blood was pouring from his mouth. Hitler picked him up and carried him on his shoulders. 'If I can only get him to the car,' Hitler thought, 'then the boy is saved.'

2     Compare the attitudes towards Hitler in Sources D and E.

# WHO WAS HITLER? WHO WERE THE NAZIS?

## What's it all about?

The Nazi Party did not exist in 1920, yet by 1932 it was almost the biggest political party in Germany. It was led by Adolf Hitler. Hitler was to become dictator of Germany and his ideas became Nazi ideology.

### WHO WAS ADOLF HITLER?

Adolf Hitler was born in Austria in 1889. After serving in the German army during the First World War, he was devastated when he heard that Germany had lost the war.

Hitler claimed that the kaiser's Germany had failed to deal with 'the problem of preserving the racial foundations of our national life'. In other words, Hitler claimed Germany had lost the war because it allowed the Jews and people of other races who lived in Germany to have too much power. He claimed that Germany had been stabbed in the back by Jewish politicians in 1918.

In 1919, Hitler joined the Bavarian German Workers' Party. At that time, it was a small group with very little money and no real political ideas apart from disliking the Weimar Republic and wanting to make Germany great again.

Hitler quickly gained influence in the party and changed its name to the National Socialist German Workers' (Nazi) Party in 1920.

In 1921, Hitler became leader of the Nazi Party. He built on its love of Germany and racist ideas to turn it into an extreme nationalist party which argued that the Germans were the most important people in the world. He claimed that true Germans belonged to a master race who deserved to rule the world.

### WHO SUPPORTED THE NAZIS?

As one of many small political groups in the early 1920s, the Nazis had to work hard to attract attention and support.

The Nazi Party appeared to be strong and decisive and it grew rapidly in the early 1920s. By including the words 'national' and 'German' in its name, the Nazis attracted the attention of nationalists. By including 'socialist' and 'workers' in the title, the Nazis also hoped to attract working-class support. The military supported Hitler's ideas of discipline and order. The middle classes and farmers were attracted by the promise of social reform. Wealthy businessmen believed the Nazis would fight communists. Some people responded to racist ideas, especially against Jews.

1   The Nazis had very vague and general aims in the early 1920s. Discuss how important the 'vagueness' of Nazi policies was in attracting support for the new party.

2   The Nazis tried to be all things to all people. Explain what this means by referring to the different groups that supported the Nazis.

## HOW IMPORTANT WAS HITLER TO THE NAZIS?

Hitler was a driving force in the Nazi Party. He was a charismatic public speaker whose speeches were so popular that they were advertised – he could even charge for admission to listen to them.

Before his speeches, Hitler rehearsed carefully, even practising the way he would stand and how he would use his arms. He manipulated crowds, often arriving late and then standing silent in front of them for a few minutes. By doing this he increased the tension. He often started slowly, but as he continued, he seemed able to reach into the inner fears and hopes of each person listening to him.

His speeches were performances which could be spell binding to his audiences. Hitler also knew the importance of keeping his speeches simple. He repeated the main points again and again, and used humour and anger to drive his audiences wild with enthusiasm.

## HITLER AND THE SA

The Nazis also used violence to increase support and to intimidate opponents. In 1921, Hitler set up his own private army called the Sturm-Abteilung (SA) or Stormtroopers. They were mostly young men, some of whom had been members of the *Freikorps*. They dressed in brown and were therefore nicknamed Brownshirts.

The SA attracted men who wanted action and that often meant violence. The SA was set up supposedly to protect Nazi meetings, but its members often started the violence and attacked the meetings of political opponents, especially communists.

Source A

A 1934 propaganda poster showing a member of the SA.

## WHY DID HITLER CHANGE HIS POLICIES AFTER THE MUNICH PUTSCH?

The failure of the Munich Putsch in 1923 convinced Hitler that the only sure way of getting more power was by legal means. While in prison Hitler reached an important decision about future tactics. He is reported as saying, 'We must hold our noses and enter the *Reichstag*.' In other words, Hitler would campaign for power legally and once the Nazis became important within the *Reichstag*, they would use their power to destroy the Weimar democracy.

1 Describe how Hitler's ideas about gaining power changed as a result of the failure of the Munich Putsch.

## NAZI IDEOLOGY – WHAT WAS NAZISM?

*Mein Kampf* was published in 1925. In it, Hitler provided very simple answers to complex problems.

Look at the diagram below.

1   Which of the main Nazi ideas would threaten democracy? Give reasons to support your choice.

2   Which of the Nazi ideas would worry other European countries? Give reasons to support your choice.

Source B

Many of the ideas outlined in Hitler's book, *Mein Kampf*, became Nazi policy.

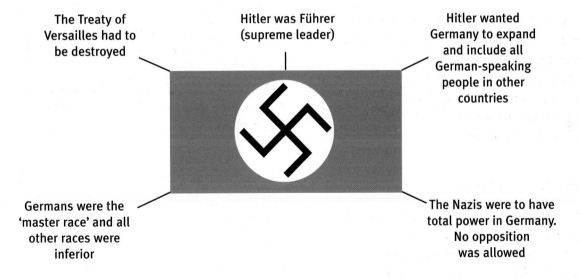

The Treaty of Versailles had to be destroyed

Hitler was Führer (supreme leader)

Hitler wanted Germany to expand and include all German-speaking people in other countries

Germans were the 'master race' and all other races were inferior

The Nazis were to have total power in Germany. No opposition was allowed

The main Nazi ideas.

## HOW DID HITLER CHANGE THE PARTY AFTER HIS RELEASE FROM PRISON?

The Nazi Party had been banned immediately after the Putsch, but two weeks after Hitler's release from prison in December 1924, the ban on the party was lifted and it was officially re-launched at a rally on 27 February 1925.

When Hitler was released, he began to reorganise the party to make it more effective in elections. He created a national organisation. Before, the Nazis had only been well known in Bavaria. Hitler knew that he needed to win as many votes as possible across the whole of Germany if he was to gain a majority in the *Reichstag*.

To spread the Nazi message across Germany, Hitler appointed Josef Goebbels as head of propaganda. His job was to put the Nazi message across as clearly as possible and, as Hitler put it, 'to defeat democracy with its own weapons'.

## HOW IMPORTANT WERE THE NAZIS IN THE 1920s?

Despite Hitler's efforts, the Nazis were not very important during the 1920s. Although membership stood at more than 100,000 in 1928, it was still difficult for the Nazis to break through into national politics. In the 1928 elections the Nazis won only twelve seats in the *Reichstag*. The Social Democrats had 153 seats and even the Communist Party had almost 50!

The Nazi Party was an extremist organisation and people only really listen to extremist politicians in times of difficulty. But between 1924 and 1929, Germany was increasingly prosperous thanks to the policies of Gustav Stresemann. During the 'Golden Age of Weimar' it would need more than propaganda and speeches to make the Nazis into an important political force in Germany (see Chapter 9).

---

1   Why did the Nazis fail to become an important national political party in the 1920s?

### ⋯⋗ *Activity*

Draw a timeline of Hitler and the Nazi Party between 1918 and 1929. There are eleven specific and relevant events in this chapter. Find them and include them in your timeline.

Use one colour to shade the time when Hitler wanted to use violence to achieve power and another colour to highlight the time when Hitler had decided to use peaceful means. Include a key explaining the purpose of using the two colours. Think carefully about when the colours should change.

---

## ⋯ IN CONCLUSION

⋯⋗ The Nazi Party, led by Adolf Hitler, was formed in the 1920s. Nazi policies were:

- ■ designed to attract attention and support by appealing to many sections of German society
- ■ anti-democratic and very nationalistic.

By the mid-1920s, Hitler had decided that the Nazis would try to gain power legally.

## PRACTISE YOUR ENQUIRY SKILLS

**Study the sources in this chapter carefully and answer the questions which follow. You should use your own knowledge where appropriate.**

In **Source C** Hitler describes the party he joined in 1919.

**Source C**

> In the year 1919, when I met the handful of men who held their little meetings under the name of German Workers' Party, there was neither a business office nor any employee. There was no paper with letterhead; in fact, even rubber stamps were lacking. The entire property of this seven men's club consisted of a briefcase, in which the incoming and outgoing mail were kept, and a cigar box which served as a cash box.

1   Study Source C. How does Hitler give the impression that the German Workers' Party was not very important in 1919?

In **Source D** Hitler describes the Nazi Party in 1929.

**Source D**

> We are on the way to power. The Party is national. The Party is heard of everywhere. Thousands of uniformed members march behind our flag and millions more vote for us. Our time has come! We can and will save Germany from the corruption of democratic politicians!

2   Compare Hitler's descriptions of the party he joined and then took over. What differences can you identify between 1919 and 1929?

3   How reliable are the sources as accurate evidence of the rise of the Nazi Party?

#  9 THE GOLDEN AGE OF WEIMAR

## What's it all about?

The years 1924–9 are often called the 'Golden Age of Weimar'.
They are also known as the 'Stresemann Years' after the most
important politician in Germany at the time – Gustav Stresemann.

### Glossary

**golden age:** a time when things go well and
people feel happier

### Source A

Gustav Stresemann.

## STRESEMANN AND THE ECONOMY

As chancellor, Gustav Stresemann was
responsible for helping the German
economy recover from collapse (see
Chapter 6). He brought hyperinflation
under control by ordering all the old bank
notes to be collected and destroyed. He
then organised the issue of a new currency,
called the Rentenmark.

Germany's economic recovery was also helped by
loans of money from the USA, which were part
of the Dawes Plan of 1924, named after the
American Charles Dawes, who organised the
loans to help bring economic stability to Europe.

As a result of the US loans and foreign
investments now coming into Germany, the
economic problems of 1919–23 faded and
Germany started to recover. German people once
again had jobs and wages to spend.

As part of the Dawes Plan, Stresemann was able
to negotiate to reduce the German reparation
payments and gave Germany longer to pay them.
At the same time the French and Belgians agreed
to leave the Ruhr and German industry got going
again. Later, in 1929, Stresemann reached another
agreement (the Young Plan) with the USA to
reduce reparation payments further.

## STRESEMANN AND INTERNATIONAL RELATIONS

When Stresemann became foreign minister,
he worked hard to regain international respect
for Germany.

In the Treaty of Locarno (1925) Germany
accepted the terms of the Versailles Treaty as they
affected western Europe, for example he accepted
that the Rhineland was to be demilitarised
permanently. At the same time the French and
Belgians agreed not to invade German territory
again. Stresemann also managed to get Germany
accepted into the **League of Nations** in 1926.

## Glossary

**League of Nations:** an international organisation set up in 1919–20 to preserve world peace. Initially, Germany was not allowed to join.

1 List the steps that were taken to assist German economic recovery in the 1920s. Explain how each point in your list helped German recovery.

2 Explain why many Germans might have felt happier with their government by the later 1920s.

## WHAT HAPPENED TO THE NAZIS DURING THE GOLDEN AGE OF WEIMAR?

When Hitler was released from prison in December 1924, Germany was very different from when he had gone into prison. The country was recovering, both economically and politically. American loans helped to create many more jobs, which in turn paid wages to thousands of Germans.

At the end of December 1924, the Nazis won just fourteen seats in the *Reichstag* elections and Nazi support continued to fall so that, by 1928, the Nazis in the *Reichstag* were reduced to twelve! Less than three per cent of the people voted for the Nazi Party.

As William Shirer, an American journalist living in Berlin at the time, wrote, 'Life seemed more exciting than in any place I had ever been … Most Germans one met … struck you as being democratic. One scarcely heard of Hitler or the Nazis except as the butt of jokes.'

## WHY DID THE NAZI PARTY DO SO BADLY IN THE THE GOLDEN AGE OR WEIMAR?

The simple answer is that the Weimar Republic was working and Germany was climbing out of the problems of the early 1920s. German voters turned their backs on political groups that wanted to destroy Weimar.

As American money flowed into Germany few voters were interested in extremist political parties such as the Nazis or Communists.

1 Describe in detail what you see in the cartoon on page 41.

2 Explain how each of the things you have described is connected to the story of Germany in the mid- and later 1920s.

3 Explain what the cartoonist is trying to say about Germany in the mid-1920s.

As life in Germany improved, few people bothered about extreme political parties who wanted revolution. Many people liked Stresemann and thought that he was helping Germany to recover.

It looked as if Germany had recovered from the disaster of the First World War and the bitterness of the Treaty of Versailles. But, in 1929, disaster struck.

■ Stresemann died.
■ The US economy collapsed with the result that loans from the USA dried up.

The Golden Age of Weimar had ended.

## ⋯⋗ Activity

1 Write a short essay explaining why few Germans supported extremist political parties in the later 1920s.

Your essay should consist of several paragraphs. Here are some tips to get you started.

■ Begin with an introduction which states the main reasons why extremist parties lost support during the later 1920s.

■ Next write a short paragraph for each of the points in the introduction. Explain why you think each reason was important and also include facts and perhaps even quotes from eye witnesses or other historians to support your reason.

■ You must finish with a conclusion. Start by writing, 'In conclusion ...'. Sum up all the reasons for loss of support that you have explained and then say what you think the most important reason was. Give a reason to support your decision.

2 Draw a simple cartoon summarising this chapter. Follow the instructions below.

■ Draw a series of steps going up.

■ Write 1919 at the bottom of the steps.

■ Write 1929 at the top of the steps.

■ Each step is to represent big events connected to Germany.

■ Plan how you will use colour to show the contrast between the events which were problems for Germany and those which show recovery.

■ Draw a simple figure to represent Germany climbing out of its problems.

■ With a partner, discuss, plan and decide on no more than three sentences summing up what your cartoon shows.

■ Write another sentence explaining in your own words why you think you were asked to do this activity.

When you have completed this task, you will have created an example of a visual summary of this unit and a method of revision which should be useful to you.

## ... IN CONCLUSION

···⟩ In this section you should have learned:

■ That the years between 1924 and 1929 are often called the 'Golden Age of Weimar.'

■ What is meant by 'Golden Age.'

■ Who Gustav Stresemann was.

■ What Stresemann did to help Germany in the later 1920s.

■ That the Nazi Party did very badly during the Golden Age of Weimar.

---

### PRACTISE YOUR ENQUIRY SKILLS

**Study the sources in this chapter carefully and answer the question which follows. You should use your own knowledge where appropriate.**

William Shirer was an American journalist living in Berlin in the late 1920s. He wrote:

**Source B**

> 'Life seemed more exciting than in any place I had ever been. Most Germans one met struck you as being democratic. One scarcely heard of Hitler or the Nazis except as the butt of jokes.'

1   How does Shirer give the impression that Germany was recovering by the late 1920s and was a more stable country? Try to find four examples from the sources.

# 10  THE NAZI RISE TO POWER

## What's it all about?

Two disasters hit Germany in 1929. First, Gustav Stresemann died. His death symbolised the end of the 'Golden Age of Weimar'. The second disaster was the economic collapse in the USA, which had worldwide effects. By 1932, six million Germans were unemployed. The economic crisis had a lot to do with the rise of the Nazis.

## NAZI REVIVAL

In 1928, most Germans thought the Nazis were irrelevant to their lives. As we have seen they only had twelve seats in the *Reichstag* at this point. However, when economic disaster hit Germany, Hitler promised that the Nazis had the answers to the country's problems. As a result, the Nazis won 108 seats in the elections of 1930. Historian A.J.P. Taylor summed up the importance of the economic problem to the rise of the Nazis when he said, 'It was the Great Depression that put the wind in Hitler's sails.'

## 'MILLIONS STAND BEHIND ME' – HELP FROM BIG BUSINESS

The year 1929 was important to the Nazi Party for another reason. In that year it received financial support from Alfred Hugenberg, the leader of the German People's Party (DNVP). Hugenberg believed Hitler could attract attention to the policies of the DNVP. From Hitler's point of view, Hugenberg was useful because he owned most of Germany's new cinema industry and many local newspapers. Through his media empire Hugenberg could make sure that Hitler gained national publicity.

Hugenberg also had important friends in big business who believed the Nazis would be useful allies in the fight against communism. As a result, the Nazis gained respectability and financial support from a number of Germany's wealthy businessmen.

Source A

DER SINN DES **HITLERGRUSSES:**

Motto:
**MILLIONEN STEHEN HINTER MIR!**

**Kleiner Mann bittet um große Gaben**

This anti-Nazi poster accuses Hitler of taking money from big business.

Hitler often claimed that 'millions stand behind me'. This might have meant that millions of people supported the Nazis, but the poster in Source A suggests something else. Was it that millions of marks from big business were the real power behind the Nazis?

1   Work with a partner. Read carefully what A.J.P. Taylor said (on page 44) about the recovery of the Nazis at the end of the 1920s. Agree with your partner on a sentence which keeps Taylor's meaning but uses your own words.

2   What do you think the designer of the poster in Source A intended people who saw the poster to think? Explain your answer as fully as you can.

## DEMOCRACY STARTS TO CRACK

In the spring of 1930, President Hindenburg appointed Heinrich Brüning as chancellor. For most of the next two years, Brüning and his advisers ruled Germany without a majority (of supporters) in the *Reichstag*. That was possible because Article 48 of the Weimar constitution allowed the president – or a person of his choice – to rule Germany without needing *Reichstag* support during times of emergency.

The democratic parties could not agree on how to deal with Germany's problems. Many people lost faith in democracy and discontent grew.

## HINDENBURG AND HITLER

President Hindenburg was a war hero, twice elected as president, but by 1932 he was an old man who was not always clear in his thinking.

However, Hindenburg did not like Hitler. He called him 'an Austrian ex-corporal' and feared that Hitler was a threat to democracy. He even wrote to Hitler saying, 'A cabinet led by you would develop into a dictatorship.'

### Source B

Hindenburg the war hero.

## HOW IMPORTANT WERE OTHER WEIMAR POLITICIANS TO THE RISE OF HITLER?

Weimar politicians believed they could use Hitler and so they persuaded Hindenburg to change his mind about him.

In 1932, Franz von Papen replaced Brüning as chancellor and immediately began undermining the democratic ideas of the Weimar constitution. He asked the president to suspend the power of the *Reichstag*.

When the Nazis won 230 seats in the Reichstag out of a total of 608, von Papen realised the Nazis could be very useful to his political ambitions. He hoped he could control Hitler and use Nazi support to increase his own power. He said, 'In six months we'll have pushed Hitler so far into a corner he will be squealing.' But he was wrong. When von Papen offered Hitler the job of vice chancellor, Hitler refused. He had no intention of being linked to a crumbling system with no power to change it.

Von Papen also had enemies. One of these was General Kurt von Schleicher, who replaced von Papen as chancellor in 1932. Von Schleicher tried to limit the activities of the Nazi Party, but in retaliation the Nazis allied themselves with von Papen's party to defeat von Schleicher in the *Reichstag*.

With the support of industrial leaders, von Papen then persuaded Hindenburg to appoint Adolf Hitler as chancellor of the Weimar Republic on 30 January 1933.

Hitler had become chancellor legally. However, he was far from having power over the whole of Germany. There were very few Nazis in the coalition government and Hindenburg had the power to get rid of Hitler at any time.

1   Describe how democracy in Germany was weakened between 1930 and 1932.

2   Describe what happened in German politics between 1929 and 1933 which led to Hitler becoming chancellor.

3   Do you agree that Hitler gained power in Germany in January 1933? Give reasons to support your answer.

## ⋯⋙ Activity

Design a spider diagram titled 'How Hitler became chancellor'. Surround the title with as many main points as you can think of. Linked to each main point draw another leg leading to a fact or detail relevant to the main point.

## ... IN CONCLUSION

⋯⋙ The 1929 economic crisis helped revive support for the Nazis. The Nazis were also helped by important businessmen and some Weimar politicians. Although Hitler became chancellor legally, he did not yet have real power in Germany.

## PRACTISE YOUR ENQUIRY SKILLS

**Study the sources in this chapter carefully and answer the questions which follow. You should use your own knowledge where appropriate.**

**Source C** is a Nazi election poster from 1932. The words on it say, 'Hitler, our last hope'.

**Source C**

1  What did the designer of the poster in Source C want people to think and do when they saw it?

2  Discuss how fully the poster explains the reasons why Hitler became chancellor.

**Source D** was written by a person who was at discussions between Hitler and Hindenburg in 1932.

**Source D**

> Hindenburg replied he could not risk giving the power of government to a new party such as the Nazis. After discussion Hindenburg proposed to Hitler that he should declare himself ready to cooperate with other parties, that he should give up the idea of having complete power. Hindenburg also mentioned his fear that a Nazi government would suppress other points of view and gradually eliminate them. Hitler refused to put himself in the position of bargaining with the leaders of the other parties.

3  How far does Source D show that Hindenburg wanted to defend German democracy?

4  What conclusion can you reach from this source about the impression the Nazi Party had created about its support for democracy in Germany?

# 11 THE *REICHSTAG* FIRE

## What's it all about?

When Hitler became chancellor in January 1933, there were only three other Nazis in the coalition government. However, by March 1933, Hitler was well on his way to becoming dictator of Germany. A mysterious fire in the *Reichstag* building had much to do with the increase in Hitler's power.

### FEBRUARY 1933

One of Hitler's first actions as chancellor was to organise another election. He hoped the Nazis would win enough seats to form a government on their own, but he was worried about the Communist Party. It was attracting many voters and challenging the Nazis for seats in the *Reichstag*.

Suddenly, on 27 February 1933, one week before the election, the *Reichstag* building caught fire!

#### Source A

A photograph showing the *Reichstag* building on fire in 1933.

There is still debate about who started the fire, but Hitler immediately put the blame on the communists. He declared, 'There will be no mercy now. Anyone who stands in our way will be cut down. Every communist official will be shot where he is found. Everybody supporting the communists must be arrested.'

1 Explain why historians think the *Reichstag* fire was very useful to Hitler.

2 Why might Hitler have wanted to blame the communists for the fire?

3 What did Hitler want to happen to the communists?

### WHO STARTED THE FIRE?

When police arrived at the fire they discovered a 24-year-old Dutchman, Marinus van der Lubbe, inside the burning building.

In his pockets were matches and fire lighters. He said that he had torched the *Reichstag* as a protest against the Nazis. However, large amounts of petrol and chemicals had been used to start the fire, which had begun in at least 20 different places. Could one man have done that? Historians have suggested that the Nazis could have started the fire themselves as it gave Hitler a very convenient excuse to clamp down on the communists.

Van der Lubbe was found guilty and beheaded by the Nazis. To this day there has never been any firm evidence to prove that either the Nazis or the communists were involved.

## THE *REICHSTAG* FIRE LAW

For Hitler, the Reichstag fire was an excuse to start a terror campaign against communists. Within hours of the fire, around 4000 communists were arrested.

Hitler persuaded President Hindenburg that Germany was under threat of a communist revolution and signed a Decree for the Protection of the People and the State, sometimes called the *Reichstag* Fire Law.

The new law took away the basic rights of the German people. Newspapers could be censored and meetings were limited. Even private letters and phone calls could be checked. Newspapers belonging to the political opponents of the Nazis were closed down in the run-up to the elections.

## ···> Activity

Work with a partner to design the front page of a newspaper reporting the *Reichstag* fire the day after it happened. First, decide if your report will be for a Nazi or a British newspaper, then decide on the following:

■ what a good front page would contain

■ a headline of no more than six words

■ three subheadings to guide a reader to the main parts of the report

■ a report to go with each subheading

■ your assessment – do you believe your report tells the full story from your newspaper's point of view?

## THE RED PERIL

### Source B

The cartoon 'Red Peril' appeared in the British magazine *Punch* in March 1933. 'Red' was a nickname for communists and peril means danger.

1  There are four numbered features or people in the cartoon in Source B. What or who are they meant to represent?

2  Why are they important to the subject of the cartoon?

3  According to the cartoonist, what is the political effect of the *Reichstag* fire for the Nazis and for democracy in Germany?

In the last few days before the elections, the Nazis increased their **propaganda** suggesting that the communists were planning a revolution. Many people believed them and in the elections on 5 March the Nazis gained 288 seats, more than they had ever won before.

Hitler was now in a strong position. Events surrounding the *Reichstag* fire were major stepping stones on Hitler's path to becoming the **Führer** of Germany.

### Glossary

**propaganda**: publicity, often false or misleading, designed to make people believe something

**Führer**: German word meaning leader

## ... IN CONCLUSION

⤳ When Hitler became chancellor he did not have much political power. In February 1933, the *Reichstag* was burned down and Hitler claimed it was part of a communist plot to start a revolution. As a result, the Nazis did very well in the March elections.

By March 1933, Hitler and the Nazis were close to having total power in Germany.

### PRACTISE YOUR ENQUIRY SKILLS

**Study the sources in this chapter carefully and answer the questions which follow. You should use your own knowledge where appropriate.**

In **Source C** the cartoonist David Low shows Hitler 'in the pocket' of a big figure. 'In the pocket' of someone can also mean the larger figure controls the smaller. The word 'Reaction', which is written on the larger figure, means old-fashioned ideas or a fear of new ideas, especially communist ones, and also possibly big business interests. This cartoon appeared in the *Evening Standard* in March 1933.

**Source C**

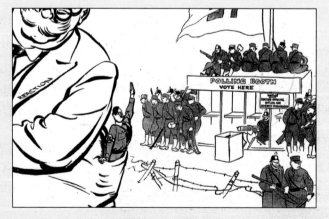

1    From what you can see in the cartoon in Source C, how does Low suggest that the elections of March 1933 in Germany were not likely to be fair?

2    Do you agree with Low that the elections were not really fair?

3    How fully does Low's cartoon explain the reasons for Hitler's rise to power? Combine what you see in the cartoon and your own knowledge to explain your answer fully.

#  12 FROM CHANCELLOR TO DICTATOR

## What's it all about?

Between 1933 and 1934, Hitler removed the last remains of democracy in Germany. He also got rid of any possible challenges to his authority when he destroyed the power of the SA in the Night of the Long Knives. When President Hindenburg died, Hitler made himself supreme ruler of Germany.

### THE ENABLING ACT (1933)

After the 1933 elections, Hitler suggested a new law that would give him complete power in Germany. The law needed three-quarters of the members of the *Reichstag* to vote in its favour, but Hitler arranged this by reaching an agreement with the Catholic Centre Party. Most of Hitler's opponents were already in prison or had fled the country, so they were not in the *Reichstag* to vote against him. As a result, the Enabling Act became law on 23 March 1933.

### WHAT IS A DICTATOR?

Hitler could now make new laws without *Reichstag* approval. Even the president's agreement was no longer needed. The Enabling Act gave Hitler these powers for four years, which meant he was now effectively the dictator of Germany.

### Glossary

**dictator:** a person who has absolute authority in a country. A dictator does not allow any opposition and the people in a dictatorship have no free speech or political choice.

### Source A

A photograph of Hitler speaking to a meeting of the *Reichstag* in March 1933.

### THE REMOVAL OF OPPOSITION

Once the Enabling Act was passed, all political parties apart from the Nazis were made illegal. Trade unions, which Hitler feared were possible centres of communist resistance to him, were banned and their leaders were imprisoned. By the end of 1933, over 150,000 political prisoners were in concentration camps (see Chapter 13).

Hitler now set about creating a totalitarian dictatorship – a system where total power would be in the hands of Hitler and his Nazi government.

1   Why was the Enabling Act such an important step on Hitler's route to power?

2   How does Source A on page 51 show the power of Hitler as the Enabling Act was passed?

3   How accurate an impression of support for Hitler does Source A give? (Read the text carefully to help you reach a balanced answer.)

## ⋯⋅ *Activity*

Hitler's dictatorship was summed up in a slogan: Ein Reich, Ein Volk, Ein Führer – One Germany, One People, One Leader.

▪ Discuss this slogan with other people in your class and create your own slogan in no more than eight words which sums up what you think a dictatorship is.

▪ Display the slogans from your class and allow everyone a vote in choosing the best one.

## HITLER AND THE SA

Although he had political power, Hitler still feared the power of the regular army whose leaders were suspicious of the Nazis. The army's leaders were very suspicious of Ernst Röhm, the leader of the Nazi Brownshirts, the SA (see Chapter 8). Röhm had a plan to merge the regular army with the SA, which by 1934 numbered over 3 million members and vastly outnumbered the regular army.

### Source B

Ernst Röhm, leader of the SA.

The effect of Röhm's plan would be to break up the regular army and put all Germany's soldiers under his control. Hitler feared army officers might be provoked into leading a revolution against the Nazis. He was also warned that Röhm might challenge his power. Hitler did not agree with Röhm's plan and used it as an excuse to plot Röhm's destruction.

Hitler's fears of a political threat from the SA were confirmed when he found out about a letter written by Röhm in January 1934.

### Source C

Hitler can't walk over me as he might have done a year ago; I've seen to that. If Hitler is reasonable I shall settle the matter quietly; if he isn't I must be prepared to use force.

**Part of a letter written by Ernst Röhm in January 1934.**

1   In what way was Röhm's letter (Source C) useful to Hitler? Give reasons to support your answer.

## THE NIGHT OF THE LONG KNIVES

On 30 June 1934, Hitler 'removed the problem' of the SA. In the 'Night of the Long Knives' Hitler used another part of the Nazi organisation, the **SS**, to kill many of his enemies, including Röhm, the SA leadership and others who had offended Hitler in the past, such as von Schleicher (see Chapter 10) and von Kahr who had helped crush the Beer Hall Putsch (see Chapter 7).

### Glossary

**SS (Schutzstaffel):** a Nazi organisation set up in 1925 as Hitler's bodyguard. It later became a powerful force in Germany.

## Why is the Night of the Long Knives important?

It was an important stage on the road to Hitler's totalitarian dictatorship. Hitler decided who was guilty and who should live or die. There was no check on his power. It is possible that up to 400 people were murdered on Hitler's orders on this night alone.

1 There are four numbered features or people in the cartoon in Source D. What or who do you think they are meant to represent?

2 Why are these features important to the subject of the cartoon?

3 According to the cartoonist, what was the result of the Night of the Long Knives?

4 In what ways was the Night of the Long Knives useful to Hitler? List at least three advantages.

**Source D**

'They salute with both hands now' – a British cartoon by David Low (3 July 1934).

Later, Hitler claimed that 61 people had been executed and 13 had been shot while resisting arrest. He said three had committed suicide. When asked why he had not taken his victims to the law courts he said, 'In this hour I was responsible for the fate of the German people, and thereby I become the supreme judge of the German people. I gave the order to shoot the ringleaders in this treason.'

The murder of suspected enemies pleased the regular army and made Hitler feel more secure. The only remaining symbol of the old democratic system was President Hindenburg.

## THE DEATH OF HINDENBURG AND THE OATH OF LOYALTY

When President Hindenburg died in August 1934, the last part of Germany's democratic constitution died also. As soon as Hindenburg was dead, Hitler took on the roles of president and chancellor and merged them to become Führer – the supreme ruler of Germany.

Hitler also arranged for every individual member of the armed forces to take an oath of loyalty to Hitler personally. The result was that, by August 1934, Hitler had complete power in Germany.

### ⋯⋗ Activity

Design a diagram showing the increase in Hitler's power between 1933 and 1934. Your diagram is a revision aid which requires you to decide on the most important developments in Hitler's power.

It can be in any form you choose, but it must have an appropriate heading clearly marked.

You should include all relevant events or themes – but don't fill it with too much detail. Remember, you must deal with all of 1933 and 1934, so do not limit yourself only to this chapter.

## ... IN CONCLUSION

⋯⋗ The Enabling Act gave Hitler almost complete power over Germany. Political opposition to the Nazis was banned. In the Night of the Long Knives, Hitler took revenge on his enemies. When Hindenburg died, Hitler became Führer of Germany. His path to dictatorship was complete.

## PRACTISE YOUR ENQUIRY SKILLS

**Study the sources in this chapter carefully and answer the questions which follow. You should use your own knowledge where appropriate.**

**Source E** is taken from an interview with Erich Kempka, Hitler's chauffeur in June 1934.

**Source E**

> Hitler entered the hotel room where Edmund Heines (an SA officer) was staying. I heard him shout: 'Heines, if you are not dressed in five minutes I'll have you shot on the spot!' Hitler entered Röhm's bedroom with a whip in his hand. Behind him were two detectives with pistols at the ready. He spat out the words; 'Röhm, you are under arrest.'

Albert Speer, Minister of Armaments, met with Adolf Hitler the day after the Night of the Long Knives. He wrote about the meeting in his book *Inside the Third Reich*. In **Source F** he describes the meeting.

**Source F**

> Hitler was extremely excited and convinced that he had come through a great danger. He described how he had forced his way into the Hotel Hanselmayer: 'We were unarmed, imagine, and didn't know whether or not those swine might have armed guards to use against us.' 'I alone was able to solve this problem. No one else!' (*Inside the Third Reich*)

To what extent does Source E disagree with Source F about Hitler's actions during the Night of the Long Knives?

# 13  INTIMIDATION AND FEAR

## What's it all about?

The Nazis used a combination of reward and intimidation to keep control over the German people. This is known as a 'carrot and stick' policy.

## HOW HITLER USED A CARROT AND STICK POLICY IN GERMANY

The phrase 'carrot and stick' comes from an old saying that there are two ways to make a donkey move. One way is to use force and hit it with a stick. The other is to encourage it by offering it an attractive reason to move - such as a nice carrot dangling in front of its mouth.

Hitler deliberately created an atmosphere of fear in Germany, but he did not terrorise the entire German population. Hitler knew he had to keep as many people as possible happy with the Nazi regime, or at least make them willing to accept it. He wanted to prevent any opposition to the Nazis and force the population to obey Nazi laws.

### INTIMIDATION – THE THREAT OF THE STICK

Many Germans were intimidated – or frightened – into accepting Nazi control. It is impossible to exaggerate the role of fear in the Nazi state. The most feared parts of Nazi control were the Gestapo and concentration camps, run by the SS.

### The Gestapo

The Gestapo was started in 1933 and was the Nazi secret police force. At first, its organiser, Hermann Goering, claimed the Gestapo was set up to protect Germany from political threats. He said, 'I alone created the State Secret Police Department.

1  Think about any organisation or organised group that you belong to (for example, at your school). What carrot and stick methods are used to keep things running smoothly?

2  Explain why the Nazis used a combination of carrot and stick methods.

This is the organisation which is so much feared by the enemies of the state, and which is chiefly responsible for the fact that in Germany today there is no question of a communist revolution.'

There were up to 45,000 people in the Gestapo. They wore ordinary clothes and often spied on daily life in Germany. Their real power lay in the number of informers and special agents they used. Up to 160,000 people were employed to inform on friends and neighbours or anything they thought was anti-Nazi.

The German people never knew when they were being spied on, or who would report what they said. But they did know that friends and relatives mysteriously vanished when the Gestapo arrived at their door.

Even in a crowd, people were alone. They kept their mouths shut and their opinions to themselves.

The Gestapo was responsible for rounding up communists, Jews and others who were considered to be a threat to the Nazi state. The Gestapo also became feared for their use of torture to gain confessions of guilt while 'questioning' suspects.

## Source A

They ordered me to take off my trousers and then two men grabbed me by the back of the neck and placed me across a footstool. A uniformed Gestapo officer with a whip beat me. Driven wild with pain I repeatedly screamed at the top of my voice. Then they held my mouth shut for a while and hit me in the face. I lost four teeth.

Ernst Thaelmann, a communist leader, was 'questioned' by the Gestapo.

1. Do you agree with Goering's reason for having a secret police department?

2. Goering seems to suggest that the 'end justifies the means'. With a partner discuss this phrase and come up with another short phrase that has the same meaning.

3. Do you agree that Nazi methods of control were (a) effective, (b) justified? (Read again what Goering said about preventing a communist revolution.)

4. Why do you think there wasn't more opposition to the Nazis' use of intimidation and fear to control people?

## The SS (Schutzstaffel)

The SS was formed as Hitler's personal bodyguard in 1925. In 1929 the SS was led by Heinrich Himmler and after the Night of the Long Knives it became a very powerful force in Germany (see Chapter 12). Dressed in black uniforms, the SS were carefully selected as good examples of Hitler's ideal master race. By 1933, there were 52,000 members of the SS.

## Source B

A photograph of the SS on parade at the Nurembourg rally in 1933.

In the early years of Nazi rule, political opponents such as communists and trade unionists were sent to the camps. Conditions were cold and harsh. Prisoners lived in wooden barracks, but they were not yet the places of mass murder they later became.

## Source C

Inside the concentration camp at Dachau, April 1945.

Himmler not only controlled the SS, but eventually also the Gestapo. As a result, the SS was heavily involved in controlling the German population.

## Concentration camps

Germany's first concentration camp was built at Dachau, a village a few miles from Munich. Originally, the camps were called re-education centres, but the SS described them as concentration camps because they were 'concentrating' the enemy into a limited area.

The camps were filled with people described by the Nazis as 'undesirables' and prisoners were colour-coded in order to identify the reason for their imprisonment – red for political prisoners, green for criminals, black for those considered to be anti-social and pink for homosexuals.

Concentration camps were places to be feared, even for 'ordinary' Germans who never went near the camps. They intimidated the German people into causing no trouble to the Nazis.

## ⋯⟫ Activity

Draw your own cartoon picture of a donkey. Make your drawing quite large but leave space to write lists at either end of the donkey.

Label the body of the donkey: 'The German people'.

Draw a stick hitting the back end of the donkey.

Draw a carrot hanging down in front of the donkey's mouth.

At the rear end of the donkey, make a list of all the things with which the Nazis wanted to intimidate or scare Germans into obedience. Title your list: 'Intimidation'.

You will return to this drawing later to add 'carrot' methods and perhaps more 'sticks'.

## ... IN CONCLUSION

⇢ The Nazis used a combination of rewards and intimidation – a 'carrot and stick' policy – to control the German population. The Gestapo and the SS were the main methods of maintaining fear in Nazi Germany. The Nazis imprisoned anyone they disapproved of in concentration camps.

### PRACTISE YOUR ENQUIRY SKILLS

**Study the sources in this chapter carefully and answer the questions which follow. You should use your own knowledge where appropriate.**

In **Sources D** and **E** George Topas, a Communist Party member, remembers his first day in a concentration camp.

**Source D**

> 'You are fortunate to have come here,' said the commander. 'This is a good camp. Here you will work and get fed. If you hand over your valuables, you will not be punished.'
>
> Just at this moment, someone moved in the ranks. The commander whipped out his gun and shot the man who moved, then continued talking without a pause: 'Now, when I finish speaking, I want you to give me all your valuables.'

1  How well does George Topas' meeting with the commander show the ways in which the Nazis used fear to control people?

**Source E**

> I and other leaders of the Socialist Workers' Party were ordered into a punishment room. It was only 60 cm by 60 cm. You could only stand upright in it – you couldn't sit or bend. I was in it for four days. I was repeatedly beaten. After four days my whole body was swollen from standing up.

2  Compare Sources D and E. In what ways do they confirm the purpose of the early concentration camps and also the methods used there?

# 14 THE 'CARROT' OF ECONOMIC RECOVERY

## What's it all about?

When Hitler became chancellor in 1933, unemployment had reached 6 million, which was almost half the workforce of Germany. By 1939, unemployment had almost disappeared.

The German Labour Front controlled most workers and the 'Strength through Joy' organisation reached into the leisure time of German families.

Hitler claimed he had performed an economic miracle but was that true? Was the economic recovery of Germany a real 'carrot' that maintained support for the Nazis among the German people?

## THE GERMAN LABOUR FRONT

Although trade unions were banned, the Nazis set up a new organisation for German workers, the German Labour Front. The Labour Front gave an extra day's holiday to its members and protected them from being sacked on the spot by their employer. However, workers had no opportunity to campaign for higher wages or better working conditions, and a worker could not leave a job without the government's permission. The Labour Front also issued workbooks without which a person could not be employed. The workbook contained a record of each worker's behaviour, timekeeping and absence rate.

> 1. How can you tell that the member of the German Labour Front in Source A supported the Nazis?
>
> 2. According to this person, what did Hitler do for unemployed Germans? Try to find four things in Source A which are relevant to your answer.

Working hours went up from 60 to 72 hours a week, but workers were earning more than ten times what unemployed Germans had received as unemployment benefit.

### Source A

I joined the party because I thought and still think that Hitler did the greatest work for twenty-five years. I saw seven million men rotting in the streets – often I was there too. Then Hitler came and he took all those men off the streets and gave them health and security and work at least for the time being.

**A member of the German Labour Front interviewed in 1938.**

## THE GERMAN LABOUR SERVICE

In 1935, a compulsory Labour Service was started, known by its initials of RAD. All men aged 19–25 had to work for the government for six months. Women were later included. Although wages were little more than pocket money, the workers wore a military-style uniform and felt that the government was at least trying to help them by creating jobs such as building the new autobahns (motorways).

## Source B

A Nazi poster advertising the German Labour Service. The caption says, 'The Reich's labour service calls for you'.

## Source C

Despite his harassed life, the businessman made good profits. The businessman was also cheered by the way the workers had been put in their place under Hitler. There were no more unreasonable wage demands. Actually, wages were reduced a little despite a 25 per cent rise in the cost of living. And above all, there were no costly strikes. In fact, there were no strikes at all.

The American William Shirer, who worked as a journalist in Nazi Germany during the 1930s.

---

1  According to Shirer in Source C, why did businessmen support the Nazis?

2  Does Shirer hint that life for German workers got better or worse? Use evidence from the source to support your decision.

## STRENGTH THROUGH JOY

The Nazis also controlled the leisure time of German workers through the Strength through Joy organisation – *Kraft durch Freude*, known as KdF. The offer of cheap holidays was a good way to attract support, and for members of KdF two cruise ships were built to take them to places such as Madeira, the Canary Islands and the coastline of Norway. In 1938, over 180,000 people went on such cruises.

Each week Strength through Joy organised leisure activities for workers, such as theatre outings and hiking expeditions. These were very popular. Sports facilities were built and there was even the 'carrot' of a possible foreign holiday in Italy. In fact, Hitler even promised every German worker an affordable family car – a people's car; in German, the Volkswagen.

Designed by Ferdinand Porsche, a Volkswagen was the dream for workers who paid 5 marks a week into a special account. However, no one received a car. The millions of marks invested by workers were redirected into weapons factories, but no one dared to complain. The secret police were always listening for protests and the concentration camps were waiting for new inmates.

## DID HITLER REALLY PERFORM AN ECONOMIC MIRACLE?

Several policies were introduced which caused unemployment to drop.

- Unemployed women were not counted in the official figures. By removing women from the unemployment statistics, the number of people out of work fell.

- Out-of-work Germans were told to work at whatever job the Nazis gave them. Few people argued since the alternative was to be sent to a concentration camp.
- In 1935, Jews were no longer counted as Germans, so they too vanished from the unemployment statistics.
- Many young men were conscripted (ordered) into the armed forces. They were no longer unemployed and the need to make many more uniforms and weapons gave more people jobs.
- The Nazis also created jobs through road building schemes.

It is true that unemployment fell dramatically, but was it because of genuine economic improvements or deliberately changing the number of people entitled to be called 'unemployed'?

## GOING WITH THE FLOW

For most Germans who did not have strong political views or who were not Jewish, the years 1933–9 seemed like good years. The bulk of the German public believed that one day they would manage to get a bite at the carrot promised to them by Hitler.

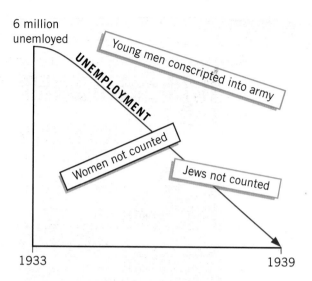

How real was Hitler's economic miracle?

Most Germans were not active Nazis, but Nazism gave many Germans what they wanted. They were prepared to go with the flow – acquiesce – as the Nazi dictatorship spread over all aspects of life in Germany. They did this because either they liked what the Nazi state gave them, or they were too scared to protest.

## ⋯⋅ Activity

Write down this heading: 'At work and play in Nazi Germany'.

Now make two lists, one on each side of a page. One list should be called 'Negatives' or 'Minus Points'. The other list should be called 'Positives' or 'Plus Points'.

Sort the information in this chapter into what you consider positive and negative things that affected the lives of Germans at work and play in the 1930s.

You can add points to your lists that are not mentioned specifically in this chapter, for example how people might feel at this time about the changes in their work and leisure time.

Now compare your lists with a partner. Is there anything on your partner's list that you want to add to your own, or ask to have explained, or disagree with? Discuss this between you.

Finally, with your partner, decide on your answer to the following question. On balance, did Nazi policies result in good or bad times for German workers? Support your joint decision with reasons, including any evidence you think is relevant.

## ... IN CONCLUSION

····> The Nazis claimed that the German economy improved in the 1930s. Although unemployment fell to almost nothing by 1939, there was no economic miracle. The German Labour Front and Strength through Joy influenced Germans at work and play.

*PRACTISE YOUR ENQUIRY SKILLS*

**Study the sources in this chapter carefully and answer the questions which follow. You should use your own knowledge where appropriate.**

**Source D** is a Nazi propaganda poster advertising the Strength through Joy organisation. It was produced in 1938 and shows the KdF travel pass.

**Source D**

1    With a partner, decide whether or not Source D is an effective propaganda poster.

2    Consider what the poster is trying to do. How are you meant to feel looking at it?

3    What impression does the poster give of life under Nazi rule?

# 15 PROPAGANDA, RALLIES AND MILITARISM

## What's it all about?

In Nazi Germany people were told what to think. Propaganda was used to make people believe what the Nazis wanted them to believe. Huge rallies at Nuremberg were an annual celebration of Nazi power, and German society became increasingly militarised with flags, drums and uniforms being seen everywhere.

### NAZI PROPAGANDA

> **Glossary**
>
> **censor:** to remove anything offensive or unsuitable

It was difficult for ordinary Germans to see, hear or read any anti-Nazi points of view. Anything that went against the Nazi message was **censored**. However, research by historians suggests that propaganda did not really persuade people to believe something they did not want to believe. Educated middle-class Germans accepted Nazi propaganda because it told them something they wanted to believe for example that Hitler was saving Germany, that Jews were wicked or that Germany had not really lost the First World War.

Hitler knew the value of propaganda. As far as possible, propaganda had to be simple, use easily remembered slogans and be repeated over and over. Hitler wrote, 'The intelligence of the masses is small. Their forgetfulness is great. They must be told the same thing a thousand times.'

1  Explain why propaganda is not the same as advertising.

2  What type of propaganda is acceptable to you? Give reasons for your decision.

3  What type of propaganda is not acceptable to you? Give reasons for your decision.

### GOEBBELS

The Ministry of Popular Enlightenment and Propaganda was created to organise all Nazi propaganda. In charge was Dr Joseph Goebbels.

Goebbels said, 'It is the task of state propaganda to simplify complicated ways of thinking so that even the smallest man in the street may understand.' Goebbels did not add that he also saw it as his job to censor or prevent Germans seeing or reading any anti-Nazi viewpoint. In May 1933, Goebbels even organised a book burning campaign where 'good Germans' were encouraged to throw books disapproved of by the Nazis on to huge bonfires.

## Source A

A photograph showing Goebbels' book burning campaign, May 1933.

1. What did Albert Speer mean? With a partner, decide on two sentences which keep the meaning of what Speer said but make it clearer to understand in your own words.

2. Would Nazi propaganda have existed if today's communication technology had been around in the 1930s?

3. Think of a typical Nazi point of view that was 'sold' to the public through propaganda. Describe the way the Nazis might have put across the message if they could have used today's technology.

## PROPAGANDA AND THE RADIO

In the 1930s, radio was the only way the outside world could get into people's homes. The Nazis were well aware of the power of radio. By 1939, over 70 per cent of German homes had a radio, which was the highest ownership of radios in the world at the time. But it was no accident that so many homes had radios. The Nazis produced millions of cheap radios, each one with a very limited range, which meant listeners could only hear Nazi radio and could not easily hear foreign radio stations, which might provide anti-Nazi points of view!

As Albert Speer, one of Hitler's advisers wrote, 'Through technical devices like the radio 80 million people were deprived of independent thought. It was thereby possible to subject them to the will of one man.'

## PROPAGANDA AND THE NAZI RALLIES

Each year, in September, gigantic rallies were held at Nuremberg.

Hundreds of thousands of people attended these rallies, where they were entertained with mock battles and military parades.

## Source B

Hitler speaking at the Nuremberg rally, 1938.

The sight of Nazi symbols and flags filled their eyes, and thundering drums and blaring trumpets filled their ears. Then the cheering began. It was always loudest and most hysterical as Hitler made his speech.

As night fell, torch-lit parades and the use of sound, light and smoke created a magical atmosphere and many of Hitler's supporters saw him as a God-like creature.

### Source C

It was 10 pm by the time the first torchlight came and then 20,000 Brownshirts followed one another like waves in the sea. Their faces shone with enthusiasm in the light of the torches. It was a magnificent picture, the snow white, scarlet, green and black colours, the fantastic berets, boots and gauntlets in the dancing light of the torches, the swords, the flags. We were drunk with enthusiasm.

Frau Solmitz attended a Nuremberg rally and wrote this description in her diary.

## PROPAGANDA AND THE OLYMPIC GAMES

Nowadays, countries spend fortunes on trying to stage the Olympic Games in their countries, and pride and honour is felt in countries that win gold medals. It was no different in 1936 when the Olympics were held in Berlin, capital of Nazi Germany.

Hitler hoped to show the world how much the Nazis had saved Germany and restored it to being a powerful and wealthy country. By building a stadium for the games, Hitler created jobs and also impressed people with new Nazi architecture. Such buildings were visible evidence that Hitler was rebuilding Germany and making it great again.

Hitler also hoped to show the power of his Aryan 'master race' by winning as many medals as possible. He almost succeeded.

At the end of the games, Germany led the medals table, but for Hitler the games had been spoiled by one man. Jesse Owens won three gold medals for the USA and also helped win another one in the relay. He was a hero of the games, but Hitler was furious because Owens was a black man.

> 1    If you had visited a Nuremberg rally in the 1930s, what would you have expected to hear, see and feel?

## MILITARISM AND PROPAGANDA

The Nazi state was a militarist state. **Militarism** relied on propaganda to convince people that Germany should arm itself in readiness for war only fifteen years after the slaughter of the First World War.

### Glossary

**militarism:** building up respect for the armed forces – the military – and creating a belief that it is normal to increase the power of the army and to plan for war

At the Nuremberg rallies, German people could gaze in amazement at pretend battles. Marches with flags, drums and uniformed men and women also promoted a militarist image. In schools, images of the armed forces were everywhere. Even children's school timetables were decorated with soldiers. As often as possible, military situations were introduced into school subjects such as maths (see Chapter 17).

Militarism was also at the heart of the Hitler Youth, an organisation where boys were taught military skills in preparation for joining the army (see Chapter 17).

## ... IN CONCLUSION

···⟶ The Nazis used propaganda to make sure that the German people accepted Nazi ideas without question. The Nuremberg rallies promoted the Nazi image of a powerful and successful Germany to Germans. The 1936 Olympic Games were also used to promote an image of Nazi success at home and abroad. Propaganda and militarism went through all of Nazi Germany.

### PRACTISE YOUR ENQUIRY SKILLS

**Study the sources in this chapter carefully and answer the questions which follow. You should use your own knowledge where appropriate.**

Source D is taken from a Social Democratic Party report on public opinion in Germany.

**Source D**

> The most shocking thing is the ignorance of many people as to what is going on in Germany.
>
> A large section of the population no longer reads a newspaper. The population seems indifferent to what is in the newspapers. The Nazis try to turn everyone into enthusiastic Nazis. But they are ensuring that people are no longer interested in anything.

1    What is the attitude of Source D towards the effectiveness of Nazi propaganda?

2    How reliable do you think Source D is about the effectiveness of Nazi propaganda?

**Source E** was written by the US ambassador to Germany in 1936.

**Source E**

> A systematic campaign of propaganda was started to break down the resistance of those who did not support Nazism and to strengthen the enthusiasm of those already supporting Nazism. With steam roller effectiveness the Ministry of Propaganda reached out into every corner of Germany, into every part of life.

3    To what extent do Sources D and E agree about Nazi propaganda?

# 16 THE PERSECUTION OF THE JEWS

## What's it all about?

Jews in Germany were persecuted as soon as the Nazis came to power. At first, Nazi policy was aimed at persuading Jews to leave Germany, but between 1933 and 1939 persecution of Jews got worse. Persecution means bullying people and in the case of the Nazis, actually murdering Jews. Eventually, the racist policies of the Nazis led to the mass murder of Jews, known today as the Holocaust.

## ANTI-SEMITISM

### Source A

Being a Jew is not a crime. I am not a dog. I have a right to live and the Jewish people have the right to exist on this earth.

**Herschel Grynszpan made this statement after being arrested on 7 November 1938.**

Why did Herschel Grynszpan say this? What had happened?

Hitler did not invent **anti-Semitism**. All across Europe, for hundreds of years, Jews had been persecuted and wrongly blamed for all the ills of society. However, by the 1930s, Jews were well integrated into all aspects of German society. They were full German citizens, sometimes having already fled to Germany to avoid persecution in other countries. But under Hitler this situation was not to last.

Hitler used anti-Semitism to create a scapegoat. Jews were visible targets who could be blamed for all of Germany's problems. Although they made up only one per cent of the population, according to Hitler, Jews were responsible for everything wrong in Germany. In *Mein Kampf*, Hitler blamed Jews for losing the First World War, argued that they were responsible for

Germany's economic crises and claimed that Jews were linked to communism and wanted to dominate the world.

### Glossary

**anti-Semitism:** hatred of Jews

### Source B

**This poster advertised a Nazi anti-Semitic film called *The Eternal Jew*.**

1   In what ways would Source B remind people of the Nazi stereotypes that Jews were greedy, dirty, linked to communism and wanted to take over Germany?

The Nazis indoctrinated German people's minds with anti-Semitic propaganda.

## THE MASTER RACE

Hitler believed that pure Germans belonged to a north European 'master race'. Hitler called these true Germans 'Aryans', and ideally, they were tall, blond and blue eyed. Hitler also claimed the Aryan race was being weakened by the influence of Jews in Germany. He claimed it was the duty of true Germans to help get rid of all Jews.

## INDOCTRINATION

As Hitler's power grew in Germany, so he wanted to **indoctrinate** (brainwash) Germans into hating and fearing Jews. The aim was to make Germans believe that Nazi propaganda against Jews was really how they felt themselves (see Chapter 15).

In school books, newspapers and films Nazi images of Jews reinforced the idea that Jews were a threat to Germany. Even children's story books had anti-Semitic messages in them.

## *Glossary*

**indoctrination:** controlling how people think and feel about something

## Source C

The sign in this picture, which appeared in a German children's story book, reads, 'Jews are not wanted here'.

## THE PERSECUTION BEGINS

Nazi propaganda against the Jews started to work. Jews were persecuted almost from the moment Hitler came to power.

The campaign started on 1 April 1933, when a one-day boycott of Jewish-owned shops took place. Brownshirted members of the SA stood outside Jewish shops to make sure the boycott was successful.

## Source D

In front of each Jewish shop were two or three large Nazis standing blocking the door. On every Jewish shop was plastered a large notice warning the public not to buy in Jewish shops.

**The wife of the British Ambassador to Germany wrote a letter to her mother about the boycott of Jewish shops (April 1933).**

In 1933, Jews were also stopped from being civil servants or lawyers. Many shops and restaurants refused to serve Jews. Signs saying 'Jews not admitted' began to appear and in some areas Jews were banned from public parks and swimming pools. Synagogues were vandalised and Jewish people were attacked in the street.

## Source E

In the centre of the road a young girl was being brutally pushed and shoved. Her head had been shaved clean of hair and she was wearing a placard across her breast. We followed her for a moment, watching the crowd insult her. My brother asked what was the matter. We were told that she had been dating a Jew.

**Martha Dodd lived in Germany in the 1930s and witnessed this scene in 1939. She wrote about it in *My Years in Germany* (1939).**

## WHY DID ORDINARY GERMANS SUPPORT NAZI ANTI-SEMITISM?

Remember that Jews were also German. To be a Jew is a description of a religious belief, not a national identity. The Nazis had to convince Germans that Jews were inferior, a threat and not true Germans. The Nazis used constant indoctrination and propaganda as well building on a certain amount of anti-Jewish racism that existed in Germany before the Nazis came to power.

The removal of thousands of Jews from their jobs created vacancies which could be filled by non-Jewish members of the 'master race'. As unemployment fell, Hitler's popularity grew and so did his racist, anti-Semitic policies.

## THE NUREMBERG LAWS

On 15 September 1935, the Nuremberg Laws on Citizenship and Race made life even harder for Jews in Germany. The Law for the Protection of German Blood and German Honour included the following rules.

---

**Law for the Protection of German Blood and German Honour**

- Marriages between Jews and people of German blood are forbidden. Marriages carried out abroad to get round this law are not legal.
- Sexual intercourse between Jews and people of German blood is forbidden.
- Jews must not employ in their households female people of German blood who are under 45 years old.
- Jews are forbidden to fly the Reich (Nazi government) and national flag and to display the Reich colours.
- Jews can no longer be citizens of Germany. (That meant they no longer had the protection of the law and their lives were made even more difficult, since they were not allowed official papers or even passports.)
- Jews must carry special identity papers with a large J for Jude (German for Jew) printed over their personal details.

---

1   Do you believe Martha Dodd's story in Source E? If so, how can you explain the actions of the people beating up the girl?

2   In a small group, discuss and decide which of the rules in the Law for the Protection of German Blood and German Honour was the worst for Jews. You must agree on one choice and provide good reasons.

### Source F

A photograph showing the devastation the morning after Kristallnacht.

## KRISTALLNACHT, 1938

On the night of 9–10 November 1938, an organised attack on the Jews of Germany took place. The event was called Kristallnacht or Crystal Night, after the amount of broken glass lying in the streets of Germany's cities the next day.

All across Germany, Jewish property and synagogues had been attacked. Over 7500 Jewish shops were destroyed and 400 synagogues were burnt down. Ninety-one Jews were killed and around 20,000 were sent to concentration camps.

### Why did Kristallnacht happen?

The Nazis claimed the attacks were the spontaneous actions of German people when they heard that a German official had been killed by a Jew in Paris. Minister of Propaganda, Josef Goebbels, wrote in a Nazi newspaper on 12 November 1938, 'The outbreak of fury by the people on the night of 9–10 November was neither organised nor prepared but it broke out spontaneously.'

However, an order signed on 9 November 1938 authorised the attack (see Source G).

### Source G

Demonstrations against the Jews are to be expected in all parts of the Reich in the course of the coming night, 9–10 November 1938. The instructions below are to be applied in dealing with these events:

*   Synagogues are to be burnt down only where there is no danger of fire in neighbouring buildings.

*   Places of business and apartments belonging to Jews may be destroyed but not looted.

*   The demonstrations are not to be prevented by the police.

*   Jews in all districts, especially the rich, are to be arrested.

Instructions for measures against Jews November 9, 1938.

1  Do you agree with Goebbel's explanation of why Kristallnacht happened? Give reasons to support your answer.

## COULD JEWS ESCAPE FROM GERMANY?

Hitler attempted to make life so unpleasant for Jews in Germany that they would emigrate. After Kristallnacht, the numbers of Jews trying to emigrate from Germany increased. Between 1933 and 1939, 250,000 Jews, approximately half the Jewish population of Germany, left the country. More would have left, but since they were unable to take possessions or money with them, many Jews were fearful of starting a new life elsewhere with nothing. Another reason why more did not leave was because anti-Semitism existed in other countries. These countries did not want to take in thousands of refugees, or asylum seekers, as they would be called today.

## FROM PERSECUTION TO EXTERMINATION

By 1939, the desire of the Nazis to wipe out the Jews of Germany was clear. On 31 October 1939, a leading Nazi, Julius Streicher, declared, 'The victory will be only entirely and finally achieved when the whole world is free of Jews.'

During the Second World War, the Nazis developed the technology to murder millions of Jews in Europe. This was the beginning of the Final Solution, also known as the Holocaust, in which the Nazis tried to wipe out the entire Jewish population of Europe, an estimated 11 million people.

Jews were housed in **ghettos** and were then sent to concentration and extermination camps. At Auschwitz extermination camp,

the gas chambers used to murder people held 2000 people at a time. With the introduction of a cyanide-based gas, Zyklon B, all 2000 occupants could be killed in five minutes.

The Nazis also murdered gypsies, Jehovah's Witnesses, communists, homosexuals and people who were mentally and physically disabled. However, the Nazis did not try to totally wipe out these groups. Only the Jews were to be destroyed completely. The suffering of the Jewish people and other groups persecuted by the Nazis did not end until Allied armies defeated the Nazis in 1945. By this time around six million Jews had been killed during the holocaust.

### ⋯∴ *Activity*

Work with a partner.

Design a wordsearch no larger than ten squares by ten squares. Your puzzle must contain eight main words or phrases linked to the content of this chapter.

The words/phrases can go in any direction and phrases can be split.

Each word/phrase must have a definition or clue to help someone find it.

When you have created your wordsearch, exchange it with another group and use the clues to find the words in their puzzle.

1  Can events in history, for example the persecution of Jews in Nazi Germany from 1933 onwards, provide any warnings to us about the present and future?

### *Glossary*

**ghetto:** an area where Jews were made to live apart from other people

## ... IN CONCLUSION

···⟶ The Nazis blamed the Jews for all Germany's problems and indoctrinated the German public with anti-Semitic ideas. Jews were increasingly persecuted throughout the 1930s. At first, Hitler aimed to force Jews out of Germany, but by 1939 plans were being made to destroy all Jews wherever the Nazis could find them – the 'Final Solution'.

### *PRACTISE YOUR ENQUIRY SKILLS*

**Study the sources in this chapter carefully and answer the questions which follow. You should use your own knowledge where appropriate.**

**Source H** was written in Leipzig, a German city, in November 1938.

**Source H**

> In one of the Jewish areas of town an 18-year-old boy was hurled from a three-storey window to land with both legs broken on a street littered with burning beds.
> The main streets of the city were a positive litter of shattered plate glass. All of the synagogues were gutted by flames. No attempts on the part of the fire brigade were made to extinguish the fire. Many male German Jews have been sent to concentration camps.

1    In what ways does Source H show anti-Semitic persecution in Nazi Germany?

2    How useful is this source as evidence of the events of Kristallnacht?

In **Source I** the American Consul in Leipzig in November 1938, David Buffum, questioned whether most Germans approved of what was happening.

**Source I**

> The shattering of shop windows, looting of stores and dwellings of Jews took place in the early hours of 10 November 1938, and was hailed in the Nazi press as a 'spontaneous wave of anger throughout Germany'. So far as a very high percentage of the German population is concerned, a state of anger that would spontaneously lead to such attacks on Jews can be considered non-existent. On the contrary, in viewing the ruins all of the local crowds observed were obviously shocked over what had happened.

3    How far do Buffum's views and the Nazi press report mentioned by Buffum agree about Kristallnacht?

4    If Buffum is correct in thinking many Germans did not support the attacks on Jews, why did persecution of Jews continue?

# 17 EDUCATION

## What's it all about?

In schools, young Germans were taught to be good Nazis. Out of school, youth organisations such as the Hitler Youth and the League of German Maidens continued the work of turning Germany's youth into supporters of Hitler and the Nazis. Boys were trained for military service while the focus of girls' education was to turn them into good mothers of the future 'master race'.

### PLANNING FOR THE FUTURE

In December 1936, Hitler stated, 'All German youth is to be organised within the Hitler Youth. German youth shall be educated physically, intellectually and morally in the spirit of National Socialism.'

#### Source A

German girls waving nazi flags and waiting for Hitler's arrival, May 1939.

Hitler knew he would never gain the support of all Germany's adults, but his intention was to build for the future. When Hitler was asked about adults who disagreed with him, he said, 'You may disagree with me, but your children are mine already.' One of the main aims of the Nazi education system was to programme pupils with Nazi ideas.

1   Why did Hitler place such importance on educating the youth of Germany?

2   Discuss in a small group what you think the purpose of education should be. In what ways are your views similar to or different from Hitler's?

### HOW WERE CHILDREN PROGRAMMED IN SCHOOLS?

The colouring books in primary schools made Nazi activities look attractive. As the children became older, school subjects such as history, biology and language all emphasised the importance of Germany and the German people, and stated that other races were inferior, especially Jews.

## Source B

„Die Judennase ist an ihrer Spitze gebogen. Sie sieht aus wie ein Sechser..."

This illustration from a Nazi school book shows a class being taught Nazi versions of what Jews looked like. The caption reads 'The Jewish nose is bent. It looks like the number six...'

Even maths was used to indoctrinate children. The maths question in Source C not only tested the maths ability of the student, it reinforced Nazi ideas of conflict and war in the minds of young Germans as they struggled with their calculations.

## Source C

A squadron of 45 bombers drops incendiary bombs (to start fires). Each bomb weighs 1.5 kilos. What is the total weight of the bombs dropped?

How many fires were started if one-third of the bombs hit their target and 20% of these caused fires?

*Germany Today*, April 1939.

## Activity

Work in a group of three or four.

Your target is to write a series of questions for a Nazi school exam.

Invent one question on each of the school subjects mentioned in this chapter so far, which would not only test knowledge but also reinforce the indoctrination of Nazi ideas.

Be ready to explain what Nazi ideas you are trying to teach by asking your questions.

Even at meal times the indoctrination continued (see Source D).

## Source D

Führer,

You rescued Germany from its deepest need.

I thank you for my daily bread.

Stay for a long time with me, leave me not.

Führer, my Führer, Hail my Führer.

A prayer said by school children before meals.

By controlling every part of education the Nazis planned to create a generation of unthinking, obedient Nazis ready to continue Hitler's dream of creating a new Nazi state that would last for a thousand years – a 'Thousand-Year Reich'.

## TEACHING IN NAZI GERMANY

Hitler appointed Bernhard Rust as head of German education. Rust had earlier been sacked as a teacher! Rust's first aim was to get rid of as many anti-Nazi teachers as possible and make sure that all school books were approved by the Nazi authorities. Any teacher who spoke out against the Nazis was sacked and all teachers had to attend Nazi re-education programmes.

However, not all teachers had to be Nazi Party members and by the mid-1930s over 60 per cent of teachers were not. The problem was that if they wanted to keep their jobs, and their lives, they could not voice their own opinion. So most teachers taught what they were told to teach.

## Source E

There are four or five teachers who are non-Nazis but if I went to America, Nazis will come in and there will be no honest teaching in the whole school. If only there could be some collective action amongst teachers. But we cannot meet, we cannot have a newspaper.

Dr Schuster, a geography teacher, wrote these comments in 1938.

---

1   Young children would learn the 'prayer' in Source D and repeat it many times. What ideas about Hitler would be reinforced or learned by repeating the prayer?

2   From what Dr Shuster wrote (Source E), in what ways did the Nazis try to control teaching in Germany?

3   How useful is Dr Shuster's opinion about what was happening in schools in Nazi Germany?

---

Specialist schools were set up to train Nazi Germany's future leaders. They were called Napolas and were run by the SS. To get into Napolas students had to be true Aryans, physically fit and members of the Hitler Youth.

When students left school at 18 they had to spend six months in the German Labour Service before some went to university.

Universities also came under Nazi control. Girls were not encouraged to go to university. In 1933, there were over 18,000 women in German universities, but by 1939, there were fewer than 6,000.

All Jews were expelled and people with anti-Nazi views were forced out. The effect was that many brilliant people had to leave German universities, including the scientist Albert Einstein.

The head of Nazi education, Rust justified these changes by saying, 'We must have a new Aryan generation at the universities, or else we will lose the future.'

---

Think back to the discussion you had about the purpose of education earlier in this chapter. Now explain in what ways the Nazis did or did not encourage what you understand the word 'education' to mean. Think widely.

---

## OUT OF SCHOOL – THE YOUTH ORGANISATIONS

At the age of 10 years, children joined the Nazi youth organisations and they did not leave until they were 18 years old.

Between 10 and 14 years, boys were members of the German Young People (Deutsches Jungvolk) while girls became members of the League of Young Girls (Jungmädelbund).

When they reached 14 years old, boys progressed into the Hitler-Jugend (Hitler Youth) and girls became members of the League of German Maidens (Bund Deutscher Mädel).

## Boys

Boys learned military skills such as practising with weapons and to toughen them up, they were taken on cross-country hikes and runs. One member of the Hitler Youth remembered that anyone who got a stitch while running was punished and humiliated as a weakling.

Boys were also tested on their knowledge of Nazism and all boys who passed the test were given a dagger marked 'Blood and Honour'.

However, most members of the Hitler Youth joined it because they thought it was fun and exciting.

### Source F

I think most of the other boys joined for the reason I did. They were looking for a place where they could get together with other boys in exciting activities. The Hitler Youth had camping, hikes and sports competitions. There was no direct or obvious political indoctrination. We did march in parades ... we enjoyed ourselves and felt important.

**A member of the Hitler Youth explains why he joined.**

There was also huge peer group pressure to join.

### Source G

All my friends had these black shorts and brown shirts and a swastika and a little dagger which said 'Blood and Honour'. I wanted it just like everybody else. I wanted to belong. These were my schoolmates.

**Hans Massaquoi, a young German in the 1930s.**

## Girls

Girls from the age of 10 years were taken into organisations where they were taught only two things: to take care of their bodies so they could bear as many children as possible, and to be loyal to Hitler and the Nazi Party. In a speech in 1934, Hitler said, 'For a woman, her world is her husband, her family, her children and her home.'

Girls were trained to be good wives and mothers and as such they could look forward to winning 'The Mother's Cross' – bronze for having four children, silver for six children and gold for eight children! It was not easy to get information about birth control. In fact, it was almost banned.

Even unmarried teenage pregnancy was approved of if it meant more true Aryan births.

### Source H

We were told from a very early age to prepare for motherhood ... and it was our duty to breed and rear the new generation of sons and daughters. These lessons soon bore fruit as teenage members of the League of German Maidens gave birth to quite a few illegitimate small sons and daughters. The girls felt they had done their duty and seemed remarkably unconcerned about the scandal.

**From the autobiography of Isle McKee, a member of the League of German Maidens.**

## WERE PEOPLE FORCED TO JOIN?

At first, membership of the Hitler Youth organisations was voluntary. The first Nazi youth organisation was started in 1926 and, by 1933, membership was up to 100,000. By 1935, that number had increased to 3.5 million, but did all these members join through free choice?

Certainly, many German boys and girls were happy to join, but there were pressures to conform. Some of these pressures were very threatening. A schoolteacher wrote in a letter to a friend in December 1938 that the refusal of parents to 'allow their children to join the youth organisation' is regarded as an adequate reason for taking the children away from their parents.

For those who still did not join, another pressure arrived through the letterbox saying, 'The Hitler-Jugend (HJ) come to you today with the question: why are you still outside the ranks of the HJ? If you are not willing to join the HJ, then write to us on the enclosed blank form and explain your reasons.'

By 1936, the Hitler Youth Law made membership more or less compulsory and all other youth groups, including church groups, were banned. Families of wealthier children could pay the subscription without their children taking an active part in the Hitler Youth, but even that opportunity was closed by 1939 when new laws made active membership compulsory. By 1938, there were almost 8 million members in the Hitler Youth Movement.

## ⋯⋇ IN CONCLUSION

⋯⋇ Hitler wanted new generations of children to grow up believing totally in Nazi ideas. The Nazis controlled what was taught in schools and subjects were used to put forward Nazi points of view. In the Hitler Youth organisations, boys were trained to be good soldiers and girls to be good mothers. Many children liked the Hitler Youth organisations and wanted to join, but some did not.

## PRACTISE YOUR ENQUIRY SKILLS

**Study the sources in this chapter carefully and answer the questions which follow.
You should use your own knowledge where appropriate.**

**Source I** is a poster for the League of German Maidens.

**Source I**

1    To what extent does Source I show typical features of the Hitler Youth organisations?

**Source J** is taken from G. Zienef, *Education for Death*, 1942.

**Source J**

> When I arrived, the schoolyard was crowded with girls. They looked serious as old women. Most of them were jumping, running, marching to the tunes of Nazi songs, to make their bodies strong for motherhood.
>
> A whistle shrilled and the girls gathered about an elevated platform. For fifteen minutes the girls received minute instructions until each knew exactly what to do and when to do it. There was no whining, no complaining. Everybody seemed eager and happy to follow orders.

2    What does this source tell historians about the purpose of Nazi girls' schools and also the methods used in them?

3    How typical of schools in Nazi Germany do you think this description is?

# 18 OPPOSITION TO THE NAZIS

## What's it all about?

The Nazis wanted no opposition to their rule, yet there was opposition to Nazi rule within Germany. There were several reasons why opposition was difficult to organise and the opposition that did exist was small scale and often based around various youth groups who did not want to conform to Nazi rules. However, faced with the power of the Nazi state most Germans kept quiet, whether or not they agreed with Nazi policies.

## WHY WAS THERE SO LITTLE OPPOSITION TO THE NAZIS?

### Political resistance was smashed

Within months of coming to power in Germany in 1933 the Nazis had effectively smashed political resistance.

Even before the Nazis came to power, political opposition to them was divided. Communists and Social Democrats would not cooperate in resisting Hitler. Their dislike of each other went back to 1919 when the SPD organised the destruction of the communist rising.

The Enabling Law of 1933 allowed Hitler to rule without the need of *Reichstag* approval and opposition parties such as the Communist Party and the Social Democratic Party were banned. The leaders of these parties were forced to leave the country or put in prison, and party members were afraid to meet each other to organise any resistance to the Nazis.

Newspapers which criticised the Nazis were banned, their offices closed down, reporters arrested and printing machinery smashed.

Trade union leaders were arrested and trade unions were banned.

## NO OPPOSITION WITHIN THE NAZI PARTY

After the Night of the Long Knives in June 1934, there was no opposition to Hitler within the Nazi Party.

### Resistance was unpatriotic

Propaganda also played a big part in limiting opposition. Effective propaganda messages convinced people that opposing the Nazis meant being unpatriotic and betraying Germany.

### Spies and informers spread insecurity

Nazi informers and spies seemed to be everywhere and places to meet that were once 'safe' were raided and smashed.

Even if groups of people wanted to organise resistance, the presence of secret police and the lack of communication between groups made opposition on a large scale impossible. It was also impossible to raise funds, and very difficult to have effective leadership or to communicate between groups. Any opposition groups that did exist were small and limited to friends. Any contact with 'unknown' people risked discovery by informants and spies.

## ···⁞ Activity

Using the information in this chapter so far, redesign the information into a spider diagram based around the title 'Why was there so little opposition to the Nazis?'

Decide from the information you have what the main reasons were and place them around your central question.

Link them to the question with straight lines.

Colour each point differently.

From each main reason now add two examples or explanations to help your understanding of each point. Place them further out on your diagram and link them to the point they develop. Colour each development point the same as the main point they are linked to.

1   According to Inge Scholl, why was resistance so difficult?

2   What actions did Inge take to show her opposition to the Nazis?

3   Why did Inge and others take such risks?

## RESISTANCE FROM MANY PEOPLE

Despite the dangers, there were people who took huge risks to resist the Nazis. They knew they were unlikely to succeed but felt they could not just accept the Nazi dictatorship.

### Source A

The fear of the people in the face of the constant threat of Gestapo intervention and the thoroughness of the surveillance system were the strongest obstacles. On the other hand, it still seemed possible, by means of anonymous leaflets and fly posters, to create the impression that the Nazis did not have solid support and that there was general discontent.

**One person who resisted the Nazis was Inge Scholl. She described the difficulties of resistance in *Students Against Tyranny*, 1952.**

## The Edelweiss Pirates

The Edelweiss Pirates were groups of young Germans who refused to cooperate with the Nazi state. They almost entirely consisted of working-class boys and girls aged 14–18 years who did not want to take part in the activities of the Hitler Youth and instead formed gangs hostile to the Nazis. These gangs had names such as the 'Roving Dudes' and the 'Navajos'. The gangs usually contained about a dozen young people who knew and trusted each other because they lived or worked in the same area. In Cologne the Navajos sheltered army deserters and concentration camp escapees.

One Edelweiss slogan was 'Eternal war on the Hitler Youth'. The Pirates specialised in attacking Hitler Youth hiking and camping groups in the countryside and Hitler Youth patrols in the towns.

### Source B

Hitler's power may lay us low,

And keep us locked in chains,

But we will smash the chains one day,

We'll be free again.

We've got the fists and we can fight,

We've got the knives and we'll get them out.

We want freedom, don't we boys?

**Song of the Edelweiss Pirates.**

## The Meuten

Other types of anti-Nazi gangs also existed. In some of the cities where communist support had been strong, gangs with more anti-Nazi political aims emerged. They were called 'Meuten' (which means 'Packs'). In the city of Leipzig, the Gestapo estimated there were 1500 Meuten members between 1937 and 1939. Since the Meuten gangs aimed to destroy Nazi control, they faced more ruthless attacks by the Nazis than some of the other youth groups.

## The Swing Kids

**Source C**

This is a still from the 1993 film *The Swing Kids*. The film tells the story of the anti-Nazi German teenagers.

The Swing Kids loved listening and dancing to swing music. This was forbidden, partly because the Nazis claimed American jazz and swing music were 'black music' and would therefore 'pollute' Aryan youth and undermine Nazi teaching about the inferiority of black people. The Swing Kids tried to wear the latest American-style clothes and dance to the latest American music. They just wanted a good time and to break free from the organisation of youth imposed by the Nazis. They also accepted Jews into their groups.

1  Which of the youth groups mentioned did the Nazis consider most serious and why?

2  If the youth groups were not a serious problem to the Nazis, why are they remembered in books such as this?

3  Do you think the youth groups are worth remembering? Discuss this question with a partner and be prepared to justify your answer with reasons.

### WHAT HAPPENED TO THE PEOPLE WHO RESISTED?

Once Germany went to war in 1939, any group which tried to oppose the Nazis was treated with extreme harshness.

Many of the youth gangs were captured and tortured by the Gestapo, sent to concentration camps and even killed. On 27 October 1944, for example, eleven youth gang members were hanged by the Nazis in Cologne, the youngest being 16 years old.

## Source D

In October 1944, eleven members of the Edelweiss Pirates were hanged by Nazis in Cologne.

During the Second World War, the White Rose group was led by Munich students. They distributed leaflets attacking the slaughter of the Jews and urged Germans not to help the war effort. In 1943, most of the group's leaders were caught and executed.

In 1943, Hans Scholl was arrested. His sister Sophie was also accused of anti-Nazi activities. The indictment (accusation) shows just how small-scale some of the resistance was (see Source E).

## Source E

The accused Hans Scholl decided to prepare and distribute leaflets. These leaflets contain attacks on National Socialism. He bought a duplicating machine and a typewriter. He claims single-handedly to have prepared about a hundred copies and to have mailed them to addresses chosen from the Munich telephone directory.

Sophie Scholl admits to preparing and distributing the leaflets. In addition, she had a part in the purchasing of paper, envelopes and stencils, and together with her brother she actually prepared the duplicated copies of the leaflet. She took part in the distribution of leaflets in Munich.

The indictment of Hans Scholl and Sophie Scholl in 1943.

The fate of Hans and Sophie was announced in a Munich newspaper.

## Source F

On 22 February 1943, the People's Court sentenced to death the following persons: Hans Scholl, aged 24, and Sophie Scholl, aged 21, both of Munich, for defacing houses with slogans attacking the state and for distributing treasonous leaflets.

*Münchener Neueste Nachrichten,*
22 February 1943.

1  What crimes were Hans and Sophie Scholl accused of?

2  Do you think the execution of Hans and Sophie was justified?

3  What does their execution tell you about the Nazi state? Think as widely as you can and discuss your ideas with others before coming to a final decision.

## ... IN CONCLUSION

⋯⟶  Hitler and the Nazis tried to crush all opposition, but there was still some resistance, mostly from youth groups. Opposition was difficult to organise since Nazi spies were everywhere. The Nazis were prepared to kill opposition members even for small crimes.

*PRACTISE YOUR ENQUIRY SKILLS*

**Study the sources in this chapter carefully and answer the questions which follow. You should use your own knowledge where appropriate.**

In **Source G** Hitler is saying 'In these three years I have restored honour and freedom to the German people.' The cartoon appeared in *The Nation*, a US newspaper, in February 1936.

**Source G**

1    Describe how the cartoonist in Source G tries to show why there was so little opposition to Hitler and the Nazis.

2    Explain the contrast between what Hitler is saying and what the cartoon shows.

**Source H** is from a leaflet issued by a resistance group.

**Source H**

> We grew up in a state in which all free expression of opinion is ruthlessly suppressed. The Hitler Youth, the SA, the SS, have tried to drug us, to regiment us in the most promising years of our lives. For us there is but one slogan: fight against the party!
>
> The name of Germany is dishonoured for all time if German youth does not finally rise, take revenge, smash its tormentors. Students! The German people look to us.

3    In what way does the cartoonist (Source G) agree with the writer of the leaflet in Source H?

4    How useful is Source H as evidence of opposition to the Nazis?

# THE CHURCHES IN NAZI GERMANY

## What's it all about?

Hitler tried to control the Christian churches in Germany. While the Nazis tried to reach agreement with the Catholic church, they aimed to create a Nazi-approved Protestant church in Germany.

Some church priests, ministers and pastors accepted Nazi control. A few may even have agreed with some Nazi ideas. But many others within the churches actively resisted the Nazis.

### HOW DID THE CHURCHES FEEL ABOUT THE NAZIS AT FIRST?

Some church leaders thought the Nazis could be useful to them since Nazis attacked communists and the church hated communism also.

The Nazis also claimed to be fighting for old-fashioned moral values. Church leaders therefore saw the Nazi ideas as a fresh start after the immorality of the Weimar years. On the other hand, many church people spoke out against Nazi abuse of human rights.

### HOW DID THE NAZIS FEEL ABOUT THE CHRISTIAN CHURCHES?

Nearly all Germans were Christians, with about 33 per cent Catholics and 66 per cent Protestants. In 1933, the Protestant church had more members than any other organisation in Germany, including the Nazi Party.

Although the Nazis wanted complete control over German life, they would have faced huge difficulties if they had tried to destroy the Christian churches.

Nevertheless, the Nazis did make some attempt to start their own German Faith Movement. It involved pagan-style celebrations of nature with the sun as the focus of worship. New marriage, baptism and burial services were also developed. But mainly the Nazis tried to control the Protestant and Catholic churches.

### Source A

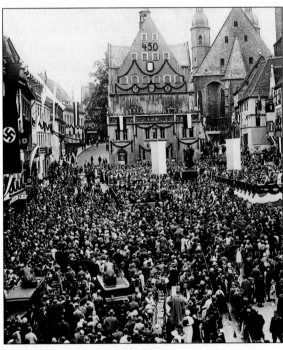

A parade of the German Faith Movement in August 1933 to celebrate the 450th anniversary of Martin Luther's birthday.

1   What evidence in Source A might prove it shows a parade of the German Faith Movement?

2   Why do you think many church leaders were torn between accepting Nazi rule and opposing it?

## THE GERMAN CHRISTIAN CHURCH

To gain control over the German Protestant church, the Nazis set up a new German Christian church led by Ludwig Müller and, in April 1933, he was given the title Reich Bishop.

In November 1933, 'German Christians' (Protestants who supported Nazism) staged a massive rally in Berlin demanding 'One people, One Land, One Faith' and that all pastors take an oath of loyalty to Hitler.

German Christians, renamed Luther Christians in 1938, played an important part in the persecution of other Christians who did not welcome Nazi rule. German Christians adopted Nazi-style uniforms and marches. The German Christian church replaced the Christian cross with the swastika as its symbol and the Bible was replaced by Hitler's *Mein Kampf*, which was placed on the altar alongside a sword.

The Nazis were also concerned about the role of Christian youth organisations and the influence they had over the youth of Germany. Since these organisations were rivals to the Hitler Youth, the Nazis wanted to abolish them. On 17 December 1933, by the order of the Reich Bishop, the entire Protestant youth movement, with more than 700,000 members, was placed under the leadership of the Hitler Youth.

**Source B**

'The Birth of new Germany'. This cartoon appeared in the German magazine *Kladderadatsch* in 1933, and refers to the 'birth' of the third reich.

1   Describe accurately what the cartoon in Source B shows.

2   How does the cartoonist feel about what was happening to German churches in Nazi Germany?

3   Explain the connection between what you see happening in the cartoon, the title of the cartoon and what you have read in this chapter so far.

## PROTESTANT OPPOSITION

There were 28 different Protestant groups in 1933. As a result, there was no coordinated opposition to the Nazis, but the attempt to control the Protestant church failed. Many bishops and pastors (church ministers) refused to give into pressure and resented the way Hitler had 'hijacked' their church. In 1934, the German Confessional Church was established by 200 pastors who believed the church should not be controlled by political parties.

### Martin Niemöller and the Confessional Church

Among the leaders of the Confessional Church was Pastor Martin Niemöller. He spoke out against Hitler and Nazi abuse of human rights. In the First World War Niemöller had become a German hero as a U-boat (submarine) captain and that caused a difficulty for Hitler. When Pastor Niemöller was arrested in 1937 and put in a concentration camp Adolf Hitler gave orders for him to be left alive. Niemöller survived the war and continued to speak out against human rights abuses long after the war ended.

Other religious opponents of the Nazis were not so fortunate. Many were held in concentration camps and several were executed, including Dietrich Bonhöffer who had left Germany to escape Nazi persecution but who returned to join the Confessional Church. Bonhöffer was a well-known writer and preacher, the sort of person whom the Nazis could not ignore. He was arrested and sent to Buchenwald concentration camp in 1943, and was executed in April 1945.

> 1   In what ways did Martin Niemöller cause a difficulty for Hitler?

## THE CATHOLIC CHURCH

Hitler was aware that the Catholic church was very powerful and, as a 'world church' under the authority of the Pope, it was not so easy to control within Germany. The result was that on 8 July 1933 Hitler and the Pope signed an agreement or Concordat. This agreement stated that the Nazis would not interfere with the running of the Roman Catholic Church in Germany if the church did not criticise the Nazis.

The Catholic church argued it had no choice but to try to make a deal with the Nazis. Cardinal Faulhaber of Munich said, 'With the Concordat we are hanged, without the Concordat we are hanged, drawn and quartered.'

### Attacks on the Catholic church

However, the Nazis soon started to break their part of the Concordat. Catholic schools were closed and priests who spoke out against the Nazis were sent to concentration camps. Catholic magazines were censored, then banned in Germany and Catholic young people forced into joining the Hitler Youth. By 1938, almost all the Catholic youth organisations had vanished from Germany.

> 1   Why was it easier to persecute Protestant churches than Catholic?
>
> 2   Hitler said he wanted to create a 'Thousand-Year Reich' where people lived, breathed and thought Nazism. Why therefore did Hitler want to control the churches?

Read the following statements and find as much evidence as you can from this chapter to prove whether they are true or false.

a   The Nazis feared the Christian churches in Germany.

b   The Nazis wanted to destroy the church completely.

c   The Nazis wanted to control the church.

d   The Nazis accepted the church had nothing to do with them and left well alone.

## Glossary

**Pacifism:** the belief that no violence is justified

## ALL RELIGIOUS GROUPS WERE PERSECUTED BY THE NAZIS

The Jehovah's Witnesses are one example of a minority Christian sect persecuted by the Nazis. Since they were without important influence at home and abroad, it was possible to take more extreme action against them than against the larger Christian churches. In particular, the Nazis were angered by the anti-military **pacifism** of Jehovah's Witnesses, who refused to do military service and resisted conscription.

Any Jehovah's Witness caught by the Nazis was sent to a concentration camp where they were forced to wear a purple triangle to distinguish them from other prisoners. About 10,000 Jehovah's Witnesses were imprisoned in concentration camps during the Nazi period and up to 5000 died there.

## ... IN CONCLUSION

···> Hitler tried to control the Christian churches in Germany. The Protestant church became known as the Reich Church. Hitler made a Concordat with the Catholic church but soon broke it. He also tried to replace Christianity with a new pagan form of worship. Many church pastors, priests and ministers died opposing the Nazis.

*PRACTISE YOUR ENQUIRY SKILLS*

**Study the sources in this chapter carefully and answer the questions which follow.
You should use your own knowledge where appropriate.**

Martin Niemöller tried to make people aware of what was happening and to stop them simply accepting Nazi control as long as it did not hurt them personally. His poem, 'First they came for the Jews', shown in **Source C**, is still quoted today when people speak up for those who are being persecuted.

**Source C**

> First they came for the Jews
> and I did not speak out –
> because I was not a Jew.
>
> Then they came for the communists
> and I did not speak out –
> because I was not a communist.
>
> Then they came for the trade unionists
> and I did not speak out –
> because I was not a trade unionist.
>
> Then they came for me
> and there was no one left
> to speak out for me.

1   According to Niemöller (Source C), why did many people comply with what was happening in Nazi Germany?

2   Is Niemöller's opinion about public acquiescence in Nazi Germany supported by other evidence you have studied? You should use your own knowledge and give reasons for your answer.

3   Discuss or debate in class:

   **a** Why do you think Niemöller's poem is still used a lot today? Is it still relevant in today's world?

   **b** Is this whole book on the destruction of democracy and the rise of a dictatorship important in today's world, or is it just done-and-dusted history? Explain your answer.

# ⋯⋮ Final Activity

This unit of study on Germany between 1918 and 1939 is part of the Standard Grade course called 'People and Power – how political changes affect people'.

The following activities sum up some of these changes.

## Activity 1

This task will help you to see the contrast between democratic Germany and the totalitarian state created by the Nazis.

Look back at the graphic you designed in Chapter 4 to show how the Weimar constitution tried to create a fair society. Your task now is to design another graphic, perhaps in the same style as before, to show how the features of the Weimar constitution that you identified as helping create a fair society were destroyed by Nazi policies and actions.

Try to colour coordinate Weimar and Nazi sets so that a point from Weimar is coloured the same as the change enforced by the Nazis.

## Longer answers practice 1

To answer the following questions, write a short essay of several paragraphs on each. You should refer to points in the graphic you produced above and your own knowledge.

1  Do you agree there were more faults than advantages in the Weimar constitution?

2  Do you agree that the Nazis destroyed democracy in Germany?

## Activity 2

Look back at Chapter 13 and your graphic of the donkey, which you did as part of an activity. Your drawing was meant to show how the German people (represented by the donkey) were forced to obey the Nazis. However, you also know by now that many people supported the Nazis.

Draw a new, much larger donkey. Copy out your stick list again and add to it at least four new pressures which can be listed as sticks and which you have found out about since Chapter 13.

Now go to the other end of the donkey. List as many things as possible which you think would qualify as carrots – things the Nazis did which gained them support from the German people. This could be quite a long list.

Finally, remember the word 'acquiesce' and what it means. Where on the donkey would you write the letter 'A' for acquiesce? Write a few words linked to your drawing to explain to another person looking at your donkey why the 'A' is there.

## Longer answers practice 2

To answer the following questions write a short essay of several paragraphs on each.

You should refer to points in your graphic and your own knowledge when writing the essay.

1  To what extent did the Nazis control Germany through fear and force?

2  Do you agree that the Nazi state only survived because most people supported it?

# INDEX

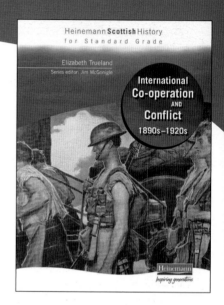

H185